"Everything is possible
Until proven impossible
And even then
It is still possible."

- John Seah

"Facts are double-edge weapons.
The great strength of knowing facts is that,
once established,
we no longer need to question facts;
The greatest weakness is
we no longer question facts."

- John Seah

PREFACE

The idea of writing this book was mooted by the 2008 Global Economy Recession. Inspired yet humbled by my experience and success of leading the Hewlett Packard team out of the 1997/98 Asian Economic Crisis, I felt ready for what I saw as necessary to consolidate our methodology and framework into a book to share with the greater audience.

I am deeply saddened by the deep retrenchment and job losses around me. Retrenchment during recession is a lousy management practice to remedy poor business performance. I hope that, through this book, managers and leaders can find new ways to do old business, new ways to revitalize existing products and new ways to reinvent the entire industry.

I write this book for CEOs, directors, and managers who believe that their years of experience have taught them everything. Many think innovation is expensive, without realizing that not innovating is even more expensive. Through this book, I hope they will see the new light and embrace innovation into their businesses.

I had the honor of being the chief judge for numerous innovation competitions. While I was delighted and amazed by some of the great innovations presented in these competitions, I shared the pains of those innovators whose projects did not make the grade. Many of these innovations either had fundamental flaws in them (which meant that their projects were doomed to fail from Day 1) or the innovators were poor in articulating the value of their innovations (which meant that they could not convince the judges that their stone was a gem). I write this book to encourage and to guide these innovators along the correct path, and hopefully, to help them avoid the common pitfalls and dangers.

Finally, I write this book as a companion guide for my workshop participants. Many of my workshop participants who embarked on the innovation journey ended up gracing the headlines of their local newspapers. Those who made it happen emerged as heroes for their companies' cost-saving or revenue-generating projects. Innovation is a journey. The incredible journey had changed their lives. Do you want to change yours?

Using the innovation methodology taught in this book, I hope that it can help you solve your toughest problems, innovate your way out of recession and fulfilling your wildest dreams.

With innovation, you do not worry about the competition.
     In your new arena, you face no competitor.
With innovation, you do not worry about market share.
     In your new market, you monopolize the market.
With innovation, you do not worry about the future.
     You create the future.

Have fun!

John Seah

ACKNOWLEDGEMENTS

I am grateful to so many friends, colleagues, and clients who contributed in various ways to make this book possible. This book narrates a journey. Along the journey, I met many friends and strangers who walked the rugged terrain with me. Strangers became good friends as we cheered each other on through good times and shared each others' burdens through the difficult times. An innovator's journey is never smooth, as conquering a new mountain is never easy.

I'd like to thank the following friends and business partners who spent precious hours reviewing the various drafts of this book. Their comments, suggestions, and ideas were valuable! They helped to shape and polish both the flow and the contents of this book:

- ▶ Foo Phang Khim, Sharene
- ▶ Leong Siew Sim, Cheryl
- ▶ Lim Hock Thye, Ronald
- ▶ Loh, Kiun Chze, Lawrence
- ▶ Tan Heng Meng
- ▶ Wong Po Ki, Joseph
- ▶ Yap Lee Yee

In this book, I mentioned a team of superheroes in Hewlett Packard who had labored very hard to conquer the Asian Economic Crisis. I deeply appreciate your dedication to innovation and your commitment to our Everest Challenge. You are the heroes behind the legacy.

- ▶ South East Asia Strategic Planning and Quality Team
  - Ooi Tay Peng
  - Ng Peng Teck

- ▶ South East Asia Product Support Team
  - Lim H C, Angelina (Business Development)

- Ngiam K K, Eddy (Logistics)
- Kok Wai Bun (Parts Supply)
- Yap Siaou Hung (Cost Saving Project)
- Kelli Yao (Finance)
- Joyce Lin (Admin)
- Hazel Lim (Admin)

▶ Singapore
- Loh Kiun Chze, Lawrence
- Goh Mia Heng, Teo Ee Tiong, David Chee

▶ Indonesia
- Yap Siaou Hung

▶ Malaysia
- Moh Siew Kee, Goh Lee Chin

▶ Thailand
- Khun Mayuree Chatmethakul, Suwat, Suleeporn, Smith

▶ Philippines
- Jopet

▶ Vietnam
- Tran, Thuan T M
- Dau Thuy Ha

I'd also like to acknowledge Goh Kheng Chuan (Rank Publishing) for guiding me through the publication of this book.

John Seah, 2009

CONTENTS

SIGN POSTING

To help you navigate your way around, I have planted the following sign posts for you, which are self-explanatory:

Key Point

Real Life Cases

Caution!

Powerful Quotes

Learning Steps

Summary Notes

SNEAK PREVIEW

"I don't see how your idea can be turned into gold."

SNEAK PREVIEW

"Now I see!"

SNEAK PREVIEW

REAL LIFE STORY 1:
THE DAY THE WORLD NEARLY CAME TO AN END

The world would have ended in 2003. Millions of us would have died. Not because of a nuclear war. Not because of a doomsday asteroid. But because of a near pandemic caused by an invisible killer – the Severe Acute Respiratory Syndrome (SARS)[1] virus.

The super deadly SARS virus was hyper infectious and it spread across the world at the speed of a Jumbo 747. Within weeks, the virus spread across the globe, infecting 8096 people in 37 countries. Okay, I might have exaggerated about the part regarding the end of the world. As the virus was airborne, it spread through cough, sneezes, touch, and even breath. Carried by wind, SARS spread through the masses across the streets and playground. Carried by air-conditioners, it spread to colleagues in the office, children in schools, travelers in airports, and patients in the hospitals. All around, people were dying. Wherever there was a crowd, there would be a danger of being infected with SARS. Doctors and nurses attending to the infected became infected themselves. As the medical professionals searched frantically for a cure, there was a desperate need to isolate the infected from the uninfected.

On 3rd April, 2003, Singapore's Ministry of Health approached the Defence Science & Technology Agency of Singapore (DSTA) and Singapore Technologies (ST) for a solution. Within a week, a prototype was up.

---

[1] World Health Organization. (2006). SARS: How a global epidemic was stopped. WHO Press.

On April 11th, Singapore rolled out the world's first "SARS Thermal Scanner", more formally known as the Infrared Fever Screening System (IFSS[2]).

And the world was saved. You and I can now live happily ever after.

Prior to this incident, nobody had heard of SARS before. How could Singapore suddenly invent the "SARS Thermal Scanner" within eight days?

What happened?

Read on …

_____

[2] A Defining Moment: How Singapore beat SARS

HOW WAS THE IDEA TURNED INTO GOLD?

Inventing a system as complex as the IFSS normally takes years. The project team needs to design, develop, build, test, and deploy. How did the Singapore team invent the IFSS within eight short days?

Innovation Strategy: To Adapt

To adapt is to make use of an existing system and adapt it to a different industry for a different usage. In this case, the DSTA/ST team adapted the IFSS[3] from a military thermal imager. Adaptation involves only minor modification, fine-tuning, and testing. That's why the innovation heroes took only a week.

More about the SARS story inside …

---

[3] DSTA. (2005). Development & Deployment of Infrared Fever Screening Systems by Tan Yang How and Team. https://www.dsta.gov.sg/index.php/DSTA-2005-Chapter-1/

REAL LIFE STORY 2:
THE CRAZY MILLION DOLLAR IDEA

A U.S. multi-national corporation was in deep trouble. The recession had taken its toll and there was a desperate need to either cut cost or chop heads. The regional director of the product service center called the staff together to brainstorm cost-cutting ideas. To encourage diversity, a cross-functional team with senior and junior staff and managers was assembled.

Having delivered his opening speech, the director left the team to brainstorm and returned at 5 pm for their presentation of ideas. He was pleased that the team had generated 3000 ideas, but was extremely angry because most of the selected ideas were outrageously crazy and impractical. "Take this for example, GET FREE SPARE PARTS," he said, reading an idea scribbled on a piece of memo pad. "Where on Earth can we get free spare parts? I am not talking about one or two pieces. To save our jobs, we need millions of dollars worth of free spare parts! Whose idea is this anyway?"

A shy junior staff raised his hand and apologized for generating such a crazy idea. Obviously there was no such thing as a free lunch or free spare parts.

18 months later, the company saved millions of dollars through the use of FREE SPARE PARTS. The crazy (or golden) idea had saved the company from retrenching its staff.

What happened?

How did the team turn this "free spare parts" idea into gold?

Read on...

HOW WAS THE IDEA TURNED INTO GOLD?

We know there is no such thing as a free lunch. Our mind rejects such crazy ideas automatically. What we need is a change of mindset. Instead of rejecting crazy ideas, we should ask, "How to?" By generating and exploring lots of possible ideas, the Hewlett Packard team managed to find a way to obtain free spare parts. Unbelievable but true, they found a source for millions of dollars worth of free spare parts.

Unknown to the product support team, there was another administrative team that routinely scrapped "faulty" new equipment rejected by customers. As these were customers' rejected products and the warranty had not started yet, they were not sent to the support center for repairs. Instead, they were scrapped and thrown into dump sites and landfills.

As part of the innovation project, the team diverted the rejected equipment to the support center and salvaged millions of dollars of good spare parts from these rejected equipment.

> Learning:
>
>> Treat all ideas as good ideas, no matter how stupid, crazy, or weird they appear at first.
>>
>> Crazy ideas can be turned into world class innovation.
>>
>> Waste can be turned into gold.

REAL LIFE STORY 3:
VOICES FROM BEYOND

Jackson was overwhelmed with excitement. He had a date with the girl of his dreams and wanted it to be perfect. He knew of an ideal restaurant to take her to, but he could not remember the name of the restaurant. Jackson called a telephone directory service. Call Agent Jane's sweet voice over the other end patiently helped him connect to the correct restaurant for him to make his reservation.

Tong was a housewife who had just purchased a brand new mobile phone. Her happy mood was dampened as she struggled in vain to make a video call to her son. Frustrated, she pulled out the warranty card and made a call to the product service center. Call Agent Mei helped her navigate through the various menu screens and taught Tong how to set some phone settings. It had been more than a year since Tong's son left to study in London, across half the globe from Singapore. She was overjoyed to be able to both hear and see her son face to face again.

Unknown to Jackson and Tong, Jane had stolen from ATM cards and Mei had cheated her company by forging her boss' signature.

What happened?
Where's the gold?
Where's the innovation?

Read on …

WHAT HAPPENED?

Jane and Mei were both serving their time as inmates in the Singapore Prison. They were working in a call center and speaking to the public from behind the prison bars[4] [5] .

What is normal then is that inmates are forbidden to talk to the public (and around the world still). How can we expect the inmates to integrate easily into the society and be a productive workforce in the society when they have been isolated for a long time from society?

WHAT'S THE INNOVATION STATEMENT?

One of the biggest problems faced by prison services around the world is "repeat customers". Many inmates released from prison were determined to change and lead a new life. However, society did not forgive them; they could not find jobs, got hungry, and returned to crime.

The Singapore Prison Services' mission is to be "Captains of Lives", motivating the inmates "to Rehab, to Renew, and to Restart". The prison officers took this problem for brainstorming to one of our training workshops. Using the techniques taught, the thought processes and brainstorming techniques that solved the problem were as follows:

Problem Statement 1:
   Our inmates could not get jobs **AFTER** they were released from prison

After Reframing, the Innovation Statement became:
   How can our inmates get jobs **BEFORE** they are released?

---

[4] Straits Time. (2005, Aug 24). 24-hour call center - behind bars.

[5] Straits Time. (2005, July 29). Sweet Female Voice on hotline.

Problem Statement 2:
Our inmates could not get jobs because their tattoos would **FRIGHTEN OFF** their prospective employers and clients.

After Reframing, the Innovation Statement became:
How can our inmates get jobs where **CLIENTS WOULD NOT SEE** their tattoos?

IDEAS TURNED INTO GOLD

The participants proceeded to generate several hundred ideas based on the reframed innovation statements. At the end of the Ideas Sorting phase, one idea stood out as the answer to both the above Innovation Statements: The FIRST **Call Center Behind Bars in the World**.

Through this idea, the inmates could be working BEFORE they were released WHILE they were still in the prison. It helped the inmates better integrate with the society in preparation for them to restart their lives anew. They were also trained on Customer Service Skills, Handling Difficult Customer Skills, and Problem Solving Skills.

CHAPTER 1
INTRODUCTION

"Now they tell me it's an economic storm."

CHAPTER 1: INTRODUCTION

> **❝** It was the best of times; it was the worst of times. It was the age of wisdom; it was the age of foolishness. It was the epoch of belief; it was the epoch of incredulity. It was the season of Light; it was the season of Darkness. It was the spring of hope; it was the winter of despair. We had everything before us, we had nothing before us. We were all going direct to Heaven; we were all going direct the other way—in short, the period was so far like the present period, that some of its noisiest authorities insisted on its being received. For good or for evil, in the superlative degree of comparison only. **❞**

Charles Dickens in "A Tale of Two Cities"

IT WAS A DARK AND STORMY DAY ...

Two memorable historical events happened in the first week of July 1997. In Hong Kong, the seven million residents celebrated the transfer of Hong Kong's sovereignty from the United Kingdom to China. The lowering of the British flag and the hoisting up of the red Chinese flag were witnessed by millions across the world.

Farther south in Asia, the 2nd of July marked the beginning of the great Asian Economic Crisis. Meteorologically, that day was bright and sunny, but the economic storm brewed out of nowhere and struck hard in everybody's heart. It was the day when billions of dollars worth of stock value were wiped out in seconds. The economic storm not only wreaked many families' rice bowls, but it also blew many millionaire investors out from skyscraper windows.

Thailand was the first country to show signs of cracks in its economic infrastructure. The banks lent too much money to finance businesses, which were not viable, and the economy over-stretched itself. The collapse in the Thailand stock exchange triggered a series of shock waves that shook the financial pillars of neighboring countries. Indonesia was next to buckle under the weight of drastic devaluation of the rupiah. Like the proverbial dominoes, the economies of Malaysia, Philippines, Hong Kong, Singapore, and South Korea tumbled and fell one after another to the synchronized rhythm of bursting hot air bubbles[6].

The Thai Baht was devalued, which triggered widespread panic. At its worst, the Thai currency plunged from 25 Baht to 97 Baht to the US Dollar. Likewise, the Indonesian Rupiah plunged from 2300 Rupiah to 17,000 Rupiah to the US Dollar. Millionaires became "thousandaires" overnight. As devastating as a massive earthquake, all the other Asian countries crashed one after another like a pack of cards.

If you had a USD$1,000,000 worth of Thai Baht in Thailand, your assets would have dropped to $258,000 overnight. If you were a millionaire in Indonesia, your assets would be worth only $135,000! As most businesses borrowed money to fuel the over-heating economy, businesses collapsed as no one could repay their loan in US Dollars (or in any foreign currencies). There were massive retrenchments and unemployment, and these triggered riots and social unrest, especially in Indonesia. Thousands were made homeless as they could not repay their property loan, and money deposited in the bank could not be withdrawn, as banks became insolvent. It was the worst recession since World War II.

Until 1997, Asia was a region paved with gold and abound with opportunities. Every direction a trader turned, every journey a ship sailed, and every cent an investor placed, all landed up in Asia. Those were the good times where businesses bloomed and the prices of cars and

---

[6] Jomo, K. et. al. (1997). Southeast Asia's Msunderstood Miracle: Industrial Policy and Economic Development in Thailand, Malaysia, and Indonesia. Boulder, CO: Westview Press.
Jomo, K. et.al. (1998). Tigers in Trouble: Financial Governance, Liberalisation and Crises in East Asia. London, UK: Zed Books.
Karunatilleka, E. (1999, 11 Feb). Asian Economic Crisis. House of Commons. UK: House of Commons Library.

houses skyrocketed. The bears were hibernating while the bulls ran wild. Things were so rosy that many people took up huge loans to finance the ever-increasing business opportunities and purchase of properties.

Asia was experiencing stellar economic growth rates of about 8 to 12% GDP. Capital flowed in from all over the world. News of mega investments graced the headlines on a daily basis. It was clear blue skies as the bubble grew and grew. Some economists called this phenomenon the "Asian Economic Miracle". I named it after the movie "The Day Before Tomorrow".

RETRENCHMENT BY DUSK

Our story began on a one dark and stormy day that July 1997 week.

I was working with Hewlett Packard (HP) as the Director of Product Support Center, South East Asia. In my close circle of friends, we joked that HP stood for Happy People as long as you could meet the revenue and profitability targets. However, if your business unit could not meet the revenue or profitability targets, then HP stood for High Pressure. Within a few days of the economic tsunamis, it became apparent that my department was not going to meet or touch the financial targets for our business. Our financial targets were set during the sunny skies days, and as good managers, we certainly needed an alternate rainy day—in this case, a stormy day plan. My business plans and budgets were drenched in the mud. I needed an alternative plan, a life buoy, or even an umbrella fast!

As if my boss had read my thoughts, the phone rang.

My Asia Pacific boss was located in sunny Australia while I was located in stormy Singapore. "Do you know that South East Asia is in the midst of an economic crisis?" he asked.

A rhetorical question, I thought. "Yes, certainly," I replied.

"I have been monitoring the situation and have done some analysis. From my calculations, you will not be able to meet your financial targets…"

Oh-no, here comes the bad news!

"From my calculations, you need to retrench 20% of your head counts to meet your profitability target," my boss said unemotionally.

Retrench 20% of my head counts! My mind went blank. I had 350 professionals with me across South East Asia. 20% worked out to be 72. To me, 72 staff was not a mere figure in our business plan. They were my friends, and I loved my staff members dearly … And … I could not bear to break the news to them.

My mind raced to find something to say to my boss.

"Boss, we planned and we executed our plans," I began. "Situations changed. We can react …"

"John, what are you talking about? This is an economic crisis! Just give me the names."

MANAGEMENT VERSUS LEADERSHIP

I was torn between the devil and the deep blue sea. I decided that this was a job for Superman.

"Boss, as a good manager, I know I should agree with you …" I paused, pondering how to complete the second half of my sentence. "However, as a good leader, when we lead our men into the jungle, we are accountable to lead our men out of the jungle." Thank goodness for my training as an officer with the Singapore Armed Forces!

"I have not changed my mind about our financial and business targets. Please do not change my mind for me," I said courageously.

"... as a good leader, when we lead our men into the jungle, we are accountable to lead our men out of the jungle."

Powerful Quotes

"How do you intend to lead your men out of the jungle?" my boss asked, dumbfounded by my unexpected reaction.

"One word, boss – INNOVATION."

There was 20 or 30 seconds of long silence. I thought my boss had died of a heart attack, or at least fallen off his chair.

"I do not know what you are talking about, John. But based on your track record, I trust you."

"Trust in your people" is one of the great virtues embedded into our brain, our life, and our work by the founders of Hewlett Packard. Collectively, these virtues of HP are known as The HP Way[7].

Whew! I was lucky that my boss did not ask me to elaborate on what I intended to do about innovation. I knew very little about innovation, apart from its spelling!

DAWN OF A NEW WORLD

What is Innovation? Quickly I ran out to buy all the books I could find on innovation and creativity. The more I researched, the more I was convinced that innovation could lead my staff out of the crisis. However, most of the books focused on solving creative puzzles, thinking tools, and memory techniques. I read 20 more books on how to brainstorm, including one that taught me how to wear Six Hats (hmm, sounds familiar). I also read a couple of books about brewing Chicken Soups with Stolen Cheese.

---

[7] Packard, D. (1995). The HP Way: How Bill Hewlett and I Build Our Company. New York: HarperCollins.

These were excellent books, but none answered my needs on how to innovate my way out of the recession.

THE VISION

It did not matter that I did not know HOW TO GET THERE, but I was crystal clear WHERE my destination was. I reckoned that I could figure out the "HOW" along the way. In the army, we were taught that if we got lost, we were to take our bearings of where we were and where our destination was. Using those two points as the general direction, we should point our compass and head towards that direction.

The Innovation Journey should start with a Vision. What is a Vision?

A Vision is a picture of a better tomorrow.

I called my team of country managers together for a meeting to decide on a vision and action plans that would tide us over the difficult times. Because a vision is about a better tomorrow, we agreed not to mention anything about the words "Recession" or "Retrenchment" to our staff. We chose to focus our energy on the upside opportunities instead of the negativity of the situation. After an hour of pondering, one of my managers came out with the idea of "BEST Service Center in South East Asia". It was a typical statement, no big deal.

What about BEST in Asia Pacific? Sounded good.

Oh, let's aim for the sky! Let us **be the BEST Service Center in the WORLD!**

Suddenly, the team burst with excitement.

The vision was inspirational.

It was captivating!

Could we be the BEST Service Center in the World?

What were the benchmarks or award for the BEST Service Center in the World?

Truly, there was no such award. How could you set a destination when there was no such place? It was like aiming to land a man on the moon, when there was no such thing as the moon. Again, we were dumbfounded.

A fruitless hour went by.

Finally, we decided that if there was no such thing as the Best Service Center in the World, we would create one. If there was no such planet called the moon, we should find a planet and call it the moon. If there was no such thing as a light bulb, then we should create something and name it a light bulb. That is what innovation is all about. To be the Best Service Center in the World, we must define and attain a target where no one had been before or attain an undisputed height that would wow the world.

Powerful Quotes

"If there is no such planet called the moon, we shall find a planet and call it the moon. If there is no such thing as a light bulb, then we shall create something and name it a light bulb. That is what innovation is all about."

I had five Key Performance Indicators (KPIs) for my service center (Revenue, Profitability, Customer Satisfaction, Reseller Satisfaction, and Operational Efficiency). My boss measured me by these five KPIs on a regional basis and I measured my country managers by these same five KPIs in their respective countries. This is called the metrics tree, where nutrients (like information, results, reports, etc) flowed up, and apples (salary, bonuses, incentives, etc) fell down.

I was accountable for the performance of six product lines across six countries (Singapore, Malaysia, Thailand, Indonesia, Philippines, and Vietnam). We used a traffic light system to measure our performance. Green light meant we were okay, amber meant we were in danger of failing, and red meant we were dead meat.

Most of the time my boss embarrassed me by calling my monthly report card a set of blinking Christmas lights. When and if I got all my Christmas lights to blink green, I called it a miracle.

To save our skin, we needed to meet 100% of our revenue and profitability targets. To do so at the expense of customer satisfaction and reseller satisfaction would be unthinkable. To do the bare minimum would not be inspirational, let alone anywhere close to achieving our BEST Service Center Vision.

Another hour went by.

We decided that a 500% growth in revenue in the midst of a recession would be world class. It sounded **inspirational**. In fact, it would be **legendary** if we could achieve a 500% growth in revenue. Surely nobody in the world could do that. Nobody would be so dumb as to choose such a target anyway. But we were not dumb; we were desperate to save 72 families. In reality, a 500% growth in revenue in depreciated Thai baht, Indonesian rupiah, Philippine pesos, Malaysian ringgit, and Singapore dollars would translate to a modest 150% revenue and 30% profit in US dollars.

Excitedly, every single one of my regional managers and country managers signed off on our vision statement and our five KPIs.

THE EVEREST CHALLENGE

Now we had a vision, but the vision itself could not bring in the gold needed to save my people. It needed to be translated into action.

How do we drive actions?

Telling the teams that if they did not innovate they would be fired was certainly one sure way to drive action. But this was not my style. Now that I had inspired (or conned) my team of managers, I needed to find a way to propagate the innovative spirit across my entire organization. I needed to touch the hearts and minds of every single employee.

To achieve greatness, we need both the Innovative Mindset and Innovative Skill Sets.

We certainly could not do things the normal way. We needed to think out-of-the-box. We needed to generate lots and lots of new ideas to:

▶ Solve our enormous recession problems,
▶ Create new streams of revenue growth,
▶ Find new ways to save cost or reduce expenses,
▶ Create new market segments and new customers,
▶ Shorten our supply chain, and
▶ Reduce logistics consumptions.

I set up an incentive scheme to encourage innovation and trained everyone on it. We formed teams both at the regional level and at the country level. Everybody's KPIs were aligned to the Best Service Center's vision.

We nicknamed the innovation journey **"The Everest Challenge"**. Everest, the highest mountain on Earth, was chosen as it is a place where dreams are chased above the clouds. It is a place where only a few daring people can beat all odds to stand on her summit. If our teams could beat all odds to achieve our 500% profitability growth target, then we would have conquered the Everest in our hearts and in our dreams.

i.   How could we innovate to bring ourselves out of the recession?
ii. How could we prosper and grow despite the worst recession in living memory?
iii. In what ways could we apply innovation to grow our business and to save millions of dollars across the organization?
iv. Could we really become the BEST Service Center in the World?

… Continue on Chapter 12.

The world's economy had been through an ever-twisting never-ending rollercoaster ride. We met the 1998 Asian Economic Crisis, followed immediately by the 2001 dot-com burst. Before the year was up, terrorists crashed jumbo jets into the World Trade Center. Just as we surfaced for a gasp of oxygen, we caught the Severe Acute Respiratory Syndrome (SARS) in 2003. The world was ripped apart again and again by Katrina, the Christmas eve tsunami, the Szechuan earthquake, the US home sub-prime crisis, Mumbai bombing, and recently the collapse of big giants like the Lehman Brothers, triggering the 2008 global financial crisis.

In the darkness of the night, there was a ray of hope. The world groped aimlessly in darkness because they chose to see darkness. One could choose to follow the world in despair, or one could choose to cling to the straw of hope. If you chose to survive the gloom and doom, you chose to persevere and to let the human mind and spirits carry you through.

How could anyone see sunshine in the midst of an economic storm?

How could we stand tall while the sky tumbles and falls?

This is what this book is about. Real life stories with real life applications of innovation. Innovation is a fascinating journey, filled with its little pot-holes and life-threatening crevasses. Embarking on an innovation journey is like exploring dark caves of unknown, filled with exciting artifacts and treasures.

Through this book, I would like to help you and your team navigate the trodden path instead of treading on virgin snow. At least, this book shares with you what's ahead in your journey so that you can be better prepared not only for the joys of conquest, but also for the heartbreaks and despair.

To find out how to bring the magic of innovation to life, read on and enjoy the journey.

SUMMARY

Summary Notes

1. Innovation is about both management and leadership.
    a. Leadership sets the directions. It takes courage to
       lead your team into the jungle. It takes commitment to
       lead them out. (Do the right thing).
    b. Management drives efficiency (Do it right).

2. Trust in your people ("The HP Way").

3. A vision is a picture of a better tomorrow.

4. The vision itself does not move mountains. It needs to
    be translated into action.

5. To be great, we need to set inspirational targets. The
    results of our achievements shall be legendary.

6. Innovation is like a journey. We know the general direction,
    but not the specific path. Point your compass straight
    and figure out the details along the way. There will be
    some points when we get lost, some backtracking, and
    some pitfalls. Strive on and we shall emerge as heroes.

CHAPTER 2
THE INNOVATOR'S
JOURNEY

"An Innovator's Journey"

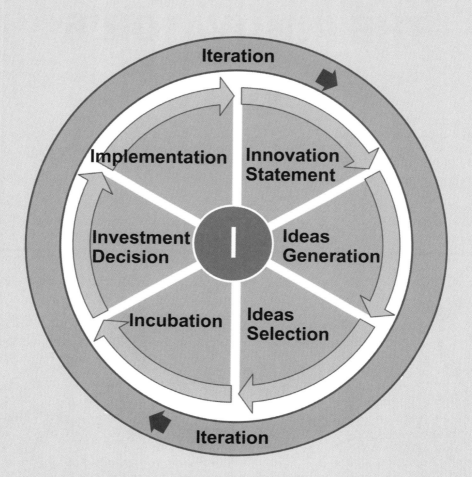

CHAPTER 2: THE INNOVATOR'S JOURNEY

WHAT IS INNOVATION?

Before we begin our journey, let us introduce two words that are often used interchangeably: **Creativity and Innovation.**

Creativity is the ability to generate lots of new ideas, new concepts, or new ways of solving problems or fulfilling opportunities. It can consist of new, novel, or different ways of looking at a problem or an adaptation of different methods of solving a problem. Creativity is typically used to refer to the act of thinking and generating new ideas, approaches, or actions.

Innovation, on the other hand, refers to the process of both generating and applying such creative ideas in some specific context. We typically use the term "innovation" to refer to the entire process by which an organization generates creative new ideas and converts them into novel, useful, and viable commercial products, services, and business practices. It is the complete process from ideation to fruition.

Key Point

Creativity is full of ideas while Innovation is full of achievements. Creativity starts with a dream while Innovation completes the journey.

WHEEL OF INNOVATION

Confucius said that the journey of 10,000 miles begins with the first step. There is, however, a Step Zero. The Step Zero occurs deep inside our heart and in our mind. Our mind must want to take that first step to begin the 10,000 mile journey.

As an Innovation Consultant, I have walked through this journey numerous times. Each time, I lead a team of different clients from different industries and I learn something exciting, something new. Each time, I found an unturned stone. I turned it and I discovered a gem.

I summarize the Innovation Journey into the following eight distinct steps, which I've coined as the Wheel of Innovation[8] :

- ▶ I (the Mindset)
- ▶ Innovation Statement
- ▶ Ideas Generation
- ▶ Ideas Selection
- ▶ Incubation
- ▶ Investment Decision
- ▶ Implementation
- ▶ Iteration

The first "I" is the most powerful "I" in Innovation. Without the first "I", the rest would not exist. The first "I" is the "I" as in "I am" or me. The "I" who wants to innovate, the "I" who wants to be great, and the "I" who is determined to take the first step in the journey of 10,000 miles. You could say that the journey of 10,000 miles begins with "I" (me).

It is the "I am" that drives the entire Wheel of Innovation. This is the hub from which all the other innovation phrases (spoke) radiate from.

---

[8] Copyright © 2009 John Seah

This is the pillar that drives the innovation project through all obstacles from ideation to fruition. The first "I" can be referred to as the Innovative Mindset.

The second "I" stands for **Innovation Statement**. It can be a dream longing to be fulfilled, a problem to be solved, an inspiration that keeps you awake at night, or a haunting nightmare to be removed. Many people called this the Problem Statement. I feel that "Problem Statement" is too narrow. It focuses only on inefficiency, ineffectiveness, or things that went wrong. An Innovation Statement, on the other hand, can focus on both the downside (problems, nightmares, crisis, etc) and the upside (dreams, hopes, opportunities, inspiration, etc).

The third "I" is for **Ideas Generation**. This is the stage where we use innovation techniques to generate hundreds and thousands of ideas. While there are hundreds of books that teach you different brain-storming techniques, I would like to share with you a few of my favorites. At this stage, we are going for volume. Not ten, not hundreds, but thousands of ideas. How long do you take to generate a thousand ideas? In a workshop of 20 participants, I only need a mere 30 minutes! I shall share the techniques with you in this book.

The fourth "I" is for **Ideas Selection**. This is the morning after. Looking at the thousands of ideas generated the day before, one would feel overwhelmed by the sheer volume of ideas to be sorted out. This is the stage where we use selection tools and techniques to filter 1000 ideas into a few really good solid ones. Different Innovation Statements require different selection criteria viewed from different perspectives.

The fifth "I" is for **Incubation**. Just like babies, the few great selected ideas from the fourth "I" are still weak and barely able to stand on their own. During the Incubation stage, we shall strengthen the selected ideas and find ways to remove their weaknesses. We can also modify the ideas, enhance the ideas or give them a practical twist. During the Incubation stage, we begin to put some thought into the ideas' practicality.

The sixth "I" is for **Investment Decision**. The selling of ideas to the management team or to venture capitalists occurs here. This is the stage when ideas and plans are developed and presented. Funds and resources are analyzed, evaluated, approved, and allocated. Based on the value and benefits presented, a critical GO-OR-NO-GO decision needs to be made.

The seventh "I" is for **Implementation**. Everybody thinks that this is the stage they are familiar with. They see it as systematic, logical, and chronological. This is, however, a myth. The challenge is to implement the innovative project in the shortest possible time with the greatest benefits and at minimum cost. Therefore, this is the stage where creativity and innovation can contribute to rapid problem resolution, tremendous saving of resources, and breakthrough ideas in the project implementation. This is the stage where gold is mined.

The eighth "I" is for **Iteration**. This is the tire that wraps around the wheel. The inner rim of the tire is connected to all the spokes. This means iteration is concerned with and is involved in all phases of the innovation project. The outer side of the tire is in constant contact with the road. This means iteration ensures that the innovation project is in touch with, is sensing, and is reacting to the changing market situation in the real world.

Iteration is not a separate stage, but an on-going stage of constantly checking: "Are we there yet?" and "Are we still on track?" It is about continuous alignment with the original Innovation Statement and Vision, keeping one eye on the project status and the other eye on the ever-changing market and customer needs.

The iteration stage is the constant reviewing of the Innovation Objective and its relevance to the environment, climate, and situation, and the alignment with the changing business and competitive environment. There may be times when the Innovation Statement/Vision becomes less relevant due to some turn of events, and needs to be adjusted, such as in the current economic crisis. What we had crafted as the Innovation Statement several months ago would certainly need to be reviewed.

Very often, iteration may bring the innovators back to Square One. Iteration ensures that if we need to go back to Square One, we should do it as soon as we realize it. And not after we have sunk in the bulk of our investments.

The respective chapters in this book are structured around the Wheel of Innovation so that you can understand, embark on, and navigate through the innovation wilderness journey better, faster, and with minimal resources.

CHAPTER 3
THE INNOVATIVE
MINDSET

"You should be proud of your daddy,
he just invented the wheel."

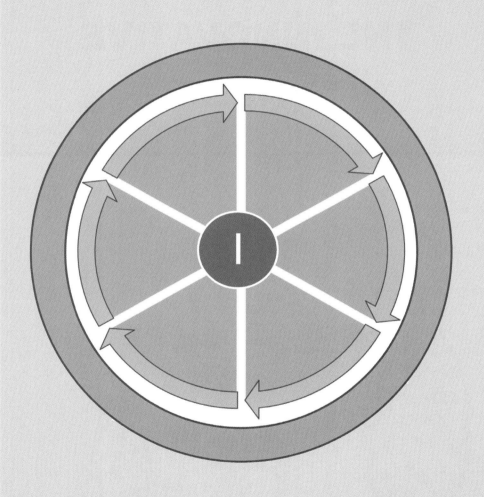

CHAPTER 3: THE INNOVATIVE MINDSET

What is a mindset? I've defined mindset as whatever you SET your MIND to be.

All of us live in this world with a set of assumptions, methods, or notations. These assumptions were shaped by the way we were groomed as a child, by the friends we mixed with, by our parents, and by the society we lived in. A child, born in a family where parents are hardworking employees, tends to believe in working hard for a fixed monthly salary. Another child, groomed by parents who are entrepreneurs, tends to believe that their money should be working hard to produce more money.

Mindset is our belief system. It determines our attitude, the way we react to the events affecting us, and how we interact with people. It drives our behaviors, our thoughts, and our actions.

In her book, the author Carol Dweck[9] stated that people either adopt a fixed mindset or a growth mindset. Those with **a fixed mindset** believe their talents and abilities cannot be improved through any means. They feel that they are born with a certain amount of talent and typically do not wish to challenge their abilities due to the possibility of failure. Individuals with a fixed mindset frequently guard themselves against situations in which they feel they need to prove their personal worth. Challenges are frequently viewed negatively, instead of as an opportunity for personal growth.

On the other hand, people that practice **a growth mindset** believe intelligence, talent, and abilities can be developed over time. They believe abilities, such as athleticism and mathematical capacity, can be improved through hard work and persistence. When presented with an obstacle, those practicing a growth mindset tend to rise to the challenge. Often,

---

[9] Dweck, C. S. (2006). Mindset: The new psychology of success. USA: Random House.

people of the growth mindset do not fear failure; instead, they view it as a chance to improve themselves.

When we embrace innovation, we embrace a growth mindset.

Using innovation as a tool and a technique, we can outrun ourselves. Combining the innovative mindset with the power of a mind, the power of a dream, and the power of belief, we can learn how to overcome fears. We can run faster and fly further.

THE POWER OF THE MIND

I jogged regularly for exactly 2.4 km every Sunday. Why 2.4 km? Because that is the distance every young Singaporean male needs to jog for our annual Individual Physical Proficiency Test (Singapore Armed Forces). Although I had fulfilled all my military service obligations years ago, the 2.4 km distance remained stuck in my head week after week. Not one step more. A few years ago, I called an old friend, Lawrence Loh, who was in his mid-forties, for a chat and found out that he had just completed his first marathon. He challenged me to complete my first marathon the following year.

It was an exciting thought. I was in my mid-forties too and I had nine months to train for the coming marathon. A marathon is 42 km long, which is a far cry from my pathetic 2.4 km weekly run. I reckoned I needed to increase my distance at a rate by 5 km per month to be ready by December 5th. I had a goal and I had a detailed plan, which I printed off the internet.

For the first three months, I jogged on alternate days, increasing the distance by a kilometer at a time. It was a mind over body game. Many times, the body wanted to stop, but the mind had to push it on. I told my mind one more kilometer. I began counting lamp posts; then I started counting bus stops. One more kilometer. A few steps more.

My job as a regional manager took me across Asia Pacific on a weekly basis. Different countries, different week. Often I would wake up one morning and wonder "where am I?" Then I would say to myself, if it is Wednesday, then I must be in Shanghai. But wherever I went, I never forgot to take along my jogging shoes. Rain or shine, I jogged. I pounded on the hotel treadmills, along dusty roads, in an empty stadium, and in countless parks. Sometimes I was chased by dogs; at other times, I was chased by crooks. I had no problem dealing with them because I outran both of them. Surely and steadily, I began to clock 21 km per session with ease, an increase of 900% over my usual 2.4 km. That's a half marathon! Four months of hard work with five more months to go, I was feeling very pleased with my achievements, considering that I had never jogged beyond 5 km during my younger days.

Then something insignificant happened. A major customer booked my December 5th date for a workshop. It was for an Innovative Visioning Workshop for his senior vice presidents and divisional directors. The date was firm and there was no way for me to move the dates of so many VIPs. I was faced with the dilemma of dropping either my customer or my marathon. Money matters aside, saying no to a customer would mean leaving the door wide open for a competitor to stroll in. The choice was obvious. Cultivating a major account took years of invested energy and I was not ready to let my competitor steal a bite off my cheese.

My marathon attempt squeaked to a halt. With the disappearance of a goal, work, customers' and family's commitments crept in. I was back to my 2.4 km jog each week.

The first phone call with my old friend planted the goal that propelled me to run 21 km. The second phone call from my client reset my run to 2.4 km.

Key Point

The ability to run a marathon is not a question of physical fitness. It is not the power of the leg muscles that propel an average busy middle-aged man to run 21 km. It is the power of the mind.

One cannot underestimate the power of the human mind. Once you set your mind to achieve a goal, your mind will drive the energy, the actions, and the schedules to achieve the goal. A mind without a goal gropes in the dark. The goal serves as the beacon of the mind to guide the ship to its destination.

THE POWER OF A DREAM

When Celine Dion sang "The Power of a Dream" in the closing ceremony of the 1996 Atlanta Olympics, a sense of awe and inspiration warmed my heart.

"It is the power of the dream that brings us here

There's so much strength in all of us
Every woman, child, and man
It's the moment that you think you can't
You'll discover that you can."

The lyrics touched my soul. The 10,320 athletes from 197 nations who gathered there in Atlanta were there because of a dream. In the pursuit of a dream, one would overcome all odds to be a winner.

What do dreams have to do with innovation?

Let me paraphrase the question in a different way. Can you name one inventor or one innovator who is wildly successful but not a dreamer? To do something great, to be somebody great, it all starts with a dream.

All notable achievements start with a dream.

Key Point

WALT DISNEY AND HIS DREAM

Walt Disney[10] created Disneyland, and it is known to people of all ages, races, and religions all over the world as the "Happiest Place on Earth". Disneyland has brought happiness and joy to many millions of people since the park opened on July 17, 1955. The standards at work at Disneyland have raised the bar for other operations. Visitors to Disney properties constantly express their high regard for Disney's overall quality, presentation, and employee performance. Because of its success, several entrepreneurs and organizations wish to do as well as Disneyland.

Walt Disney was one of the individuals who believed in his dreams. His words of advice on becoming a wise man and being successful were as follows:

Key Point

1. Think about the values you wish to live your life by.

2. Believe in yourself based on the thinking you've done about the values you're going to live your life by.

---

[10] Greene, K. a. (1998). The Story of Walt Disney. Viking.

3. Dream about the things that can be, based on your belief in yourself and the values you're going to live by.

4. Dare to make your dreams become reality, based on your belief in yourself and your values.

Walt Disney considered Saturday to be "Daddy's Day" with his two daughters. He would often take them to Griffith Park in Los Angeles for an outing. The park was large and contained many attractions that children loved. There was a pony ride, a miniature train ride, a "train town", which housed a collection of old trains and locomotives. The children could board them and fantasize about being the conductor of the grand machines. But the biggest attraction of all was a magnificent old carousel set atop a hill.

During these visits, Walt Disney would put his girls on the carousel and sit on the bench holding their popcorn and candy while he watched them ride round and round. He said the popcorn was stale and the cotton candy was limp and the employees at the carousel could not care less if the patrons were there or if they were happy or not. Making matters even worse, he noticed that although the horses on the carousels were all supposed to be jumpers, some of them did not go up and down. What's more, the paint on the carousel horses was badly chipped and peeling away in many places. That bothered Walt Disney very much. It bothered him enough to pick up his sketchpad and pencil to begin drawing and putting down his thoughts of what his dream amusement park would be like.

Walt Disney did more than just jot down his dream; he took actions to accomplish it. He believed in his dream and put his plans into actions. Walt Disney completely reconstructed an old industry that was worn out and had developed a terrible reputation. Amusement parks, fairs, and carnivals were known for dishonesty, drug dealing, and poor child labor practices. Walt Disney made the industry respectable through his own devotion to values and high standards and unrelenting quest for excellence in everything he did.

More importantly, he had a dream to achieve and he put his heart and mind into making his dream come true. Walt Disney reinvented the theme park by raising the amusement park to an entirely new level, and Disneyland now brings joy to little children and adults from all over the world.

Disney had achieved:

1)   **Product Innovation:**

From old rusty carousels of the past, Disney had transformed the theme park industry by incorporating the latest state-of-the-art technology into his rides and shows. The rides are not only fun and delightful; the innovators in Disneyland exploited technologies in creative ways to bring the element of surprise for their guests.

2)   **Service Innovation:**

From ride operators, the staff are transformed into cast members. Each of them has a role to play in delighting and entertaining the guests, over and above their duties to operate the rides.

At Disney, service innovations and creativity are everywhere, from queue management to main street parades, from jungle cruise humorous scripts to stage performances.

3)   **Positioning Innovation:**

Prior to Disneyland, amusement parks of the past had bad reputations as they were associated with gangsters, drugs, and child labor. Common accepted norm in those days were:

► Everybody could stroll into the amusement parks free of

charge; customers only paid for the ride they took. As the result, drunks and baddies came in and hung around all day.

- ■ Disney reversed the thinking and charged admission fees, and guests got to ride all day for free.

▶ "You got to have a Ferris wheel and you got to sell liquor," his friends said.

- ■ Disney did not want a Ferris wheel and did not want to sell liquor. He placed a lot of emphasis in satisfying families rather than drunken men.

▶ "It will cost you too much money to keep rest rooms clean," people advised.

- ■ Disney reversed the thinking: "Clean rest rooms attract mothers and families."

By thinking differently and using lots of creativity, Disney transformed Disneyland into the "happiest place on Earth".

MICHAEL DELL AND HIS DREAM

At the tender young age of 17, Michael Dell[11] had a dream. He dreamt of building personal computers (PC) and delivering them to his customers at a price so compelling that he skipped lectures during his university days to devote time to this dream. When his parents heard that the young Michael was not attending university (which they thought he was), they flew to his university to counsel him. "You've got to stop this computer stuff and concentrate on your school," his father said to him. "Get your priorities straight. What do you want to do with your life?"

---

[11] Dell, Michael. w. (1999). Direct from DELL. Harper Collins Fredman.

"I want to compete with IBM!" Michael said. At 18, while most of the college graduates would be happy to be hired by IBM, young Michael wanted to compete with IBM.

During those days, IBM, Compaq, HP, and all the major PC players in the world believed in the achievement of market share through the deployment of as many "feet on the streets" (salesmen) as possible through the establishment of a complex network of wholesalers and resellers. Michael Dell discovered a means to shortcut all the chain of wholesalers and resellers in the extremely price sensitive personal computer arena by going direct. His value proposition to his customers was a breakthrough.

More resellers and more tiers of resellers meant more mouths sharing the ever-thinning profit, which added up to higher prices for the consumer. To remain competitive, all the PC manufacturers sought for operational efficiency and sourced for cheaper parts and component prices worldwide. Standardization of production lines and PC models would optimize costs, as there would be fewer models to manufacture, order, and stock. Furthermore, there would be more savings through bulk purchase of standardized items.

With the launch of each new Intel chip and the rollout of each new PC model, the older models suffered a dramatic price drop. Price-slashing promotions was one of the more popular ways to clear the older stock from the warehouses before flooding the warehouses with pallets of the latest products. Accuracy of monthly/weekly unit forecasts and inventory per model was critical to the profitability and the survival of the PC manufacturers.

Consumers, then, had to buy from the catalogues of few standardized PC models (manufacturer's operational efficiency) at a high price (long chain of wholesalers and resellers.) If he needed a different configuration, he would have to buy add-ons separately and pay for the installation charges for such add-ons.

Dell's breakthrough DIRECT business model and strategy changed the way PCs were manufactured and sold. Dell's customers ordered the PC directly from the manufacturers and the orders were shipped directly to the customers, without all the non-value-added resellers in-between. Through a powerful internet engine and an efficient manufacturing capability, customers could pick and choose the configuration of their choice at a click of a mouse.

Dell's secret was that in its heart, he believed that status quo was never good enough. He said, "I still think of us as a challenger. I still think of us attacking."

Michael Dell did not invent the PC. Neither was he known for his great products or services. His achievements were due to:

Process Innovation:

▶ While his competitors, IBM and HP, were busy building and selling through resellers and wholesalers network chains, Dell reengineered the sales processes to sell direct via the internet.

▶ While his competitors were busy standardizing their products, Dell found a way to individualize the product. He was able to manufacture PCs of different configurations for different customers. This innovative process created a brand new niche market where there was no competitor.

THE TWO CYCLE MECHANICS AND THEIR DREAMS

Two cycle mechanics, Wright Orville and his brother Wilbur, had a dream. In their dream, people could fly.

They conceived an idea to build a machine that would fly, and invented an airplane (a heavier than air machine) that actually flew. What would have happened if the Wright brothers had not dreamt big? They would probably have stuck to their comfort zone to design and manufacture better and faster bicycles.

A new invention, like a flying machine, certainly took more than a dream and imagination. It required much sheer determination to overcome enormous difficulties one by one. It required courage to decide whether to invest the family fortune on such a risky venture. It required even more courage to commit one of the brothers to be on that flimsy flying mechanical contraption, at the risk of losing his life and limbs.

History is filled with many famous men and women who achieved greatness. They all had something in common. They dreamt big and they took massive actions. These great people failed too. But they stood up and they tried again. And again.

Great people dreamt big and they took massive actions. These people failed too. They stood up and they tried again.

Key Point

HOW TO DREAM – "I WISH"

As we grow up in this relentless world of adulthood, we learn to be more logical and more practical. We began to realize the limitation of what we could and could not do. We started to see things as impossible, before we even gave it a try. In another words, we learnt to stop dreaming.

But then we marveled at those who achieved big dreams. We forgot that they were people like us. Except that these people lived their dreams, they refused to give up, and they stubbornly strived to succeed. They understood the risk, took up the challenges, invested time and resources, and they overcame obstacles after obstacles.

If others can, you can too.

Remember that the size of your success is proportional the size of your dream.

A 50-year-old participant in my workshop asked me a simple question, "How to dream?" Initially I thought it a strange question. I hesitated for a while and realized that it was a very important and valid question. Many of us had forgotten how to dream. We grew up in a practical world and worked tirelessly throughout our life, attending meetings and meeting deadlines. We focused so much on yesterday, today, and the immediate tomorrow that we had forgotten about the beautiful world that we wished to live in. It seemed so distant, so unreachable. Many of us had forgotten about our dreams.

Key Point

Great people made history and left behind legacies.

What about you?

How big is your dream?

Have you forgotten about your dreams?

Or have you forgotten how to dream?

Learning Steps

LEARNING STEPS

I am a strong believer that dreams, like a business plan, must be put in writing.

Take a blank piece of paper. Begin with "I wish …" or "I dream …"

I wish I am a millionaire …
I wish I can stay in a condominium by the seafront …
I wish I can own an internet online business selling …
I dream of a pollution-free world where cars will run on free renewable solar energy …
I dream of clear safe water for every human being …

What do you wish for?

At this point, do not worry about how to achieve your dreams. The "How-To" is an action phase that will be dealt with in later chapters.

THE MONSTER CALLED FEAR

What is stopping you from dreaming big and making your dream come true?

FEAR is the word. Fear is the enemy to success. I asked a thousand participants in my workshops to list down their top fears. And these are the fear of failure, fear of friends laughing at them, fear of losing their investments, fear of not gaining enough support from their bosses, fear of lack of knowledge or resources, or simply fear of not delivering what they have promised.

During my military officer cadet days, I used to sing a song: "To conquer, we conquer first ourselves". To conquer fear, we must first understand fear itself.

▶ Fear is a natural protection and reaction to harm

Because of fear, we naturally take precaution to avoid doing dangerous things.

▶ But believing in fear harms our ability to explore

Once fear rules our lives, we no longer want to explore new ventures or try new things. We became contented and developed a comfort zone. Over time, moving one step out of the comfort zone becomes fearful.

▶ To conquer fear, we have to get to the other side.

We can overcome the fear of failure with repeated success. Try some small and safe successes first. Then take another step deeper. And deeper and bigger and bolder.

Remember the first time you learned swimming? You took one step at a time, going deeper into the pool until you were comfortable.

I remembered the first time I learned diving. I took my first plunge before I could swim. It was terrifying. I hesitated so long that the guy behind got fed up of waiting. He decided to help me by pushing me off. The one-meter spring board first. Then three meters. Then five meters. After we overcame our initial fear, the fun of diving took over and we were ready for more fanciful aerobatic maneuvers.

OVERCOMING FEAR

Years later, I found out that my diving experience in overcoming fear was also applicable in paratrooper training. For some of the people doing it for the first time, it was a terrifying experience to jump off a flying plane. To counter the fear of jumping into unknown, the training employed a one-step-at-a-time approach where the paratroopers were trained to do the following:

- ► Focus on the horizon
- ► Count one thousand, two thousand, three thousand, four thousand, five thousand
- ► Pull the cord

First, the trainees would be required to go through the few steps by starting at a low altitude. Then they would be asked to jump off from 10 meters in the next training, 75 meters in the next, and finally take the ultimate big jump. This was a step-by-step approach of overcoming the fear of jumping from sky high.

At the early stages, the rip cord of the parachute was attached to the plane, so that the chute deployed automatically after the paratrooper had dropped a certain distance from the plane. Eventually, they progressed to a free-fall jump, where they had the confidence to pull their own rip cords at the desired height.

Have you pondered?

- ► What dreams do you want to fulfill but have not done so because of the different excuses you have created for yourself?
- ► Is this dream so overpowering that it captures your heart and mind?
- ► Have you taken any initial steps towards your dream?
- ► What other steps can you take to overcome the obstacles?

LEARNING STEPS

Learning Steps

Try this simple three-step exercise to conquer fear on your own.

1. What's stopping you. Write down three top fears.

2. What's the worst that can happen if you fail?

3. What will you gain if you succeed?

Most of the time, the worst-case scenario is not as fearful after you have visualized it.

So what if your friends, bosses, and peers laugh at you?

So what if you cannot meet up to their expectations?

So what if you fail?

No big deal after all.

On the other hand, the benefits of your success will be far greater (or else you would not feel inspired to take action). By balancing the benefits of winning and the fear of losing, most of the time it makes sense to put your dreams or innovative ideas into action.

THE INVENTION OF THE ELECTRONIC VAULTING SYSTEM

I like to tease my participants by asking them "who was the world famous inventor of electronic vaulting?" They would be stumped. None of them knew what electronic vaulting was, what more about its inventor. I would insist that the class knew him and the class would throw out names like Bill Gates, Steve Jobs, etc.

In the mid-1980s, I was a young manager working with Digital Equipment Corporation (DEC). I led a team of engineers providing Data Center Services to my clients (like disaster recovery services, facilities management services (a.k.a. outsourcing), mission critical services, etc). In those days, a 1 MHz computer was the size of two refrigerators and a 256 MB disk drive was bigger than your washing machine. Today, your mobile phone has a much faster CPU speed and bigger storage capacity than those systems inside my data center.

One of my clients was a very ambitious lady, vice president in a German bank. One day, she called me excitedly and wanted to install an Electronic Vaulting System. Since I knew nothing about the Electronic Vaulting System, I called my colleague in DEC Germany. He was a senior engineer who developed the Electronic Vaulting System.

The concept involved the transmission and storage of business-critical live electronic data from the main computer into another computer system in an alternative site. If a crisis happened on the main computer site, the live banking data up to the latest transaction would have been backed up in the alternate site. Therefore the bank could recover its data and services in a matter of seconds. Today, these systems are commonly known as Information Technology Service Continuity "Hot Sites."

I asked him to forward the hardware and software configurations to me, which we sold to the customer. The main computer was installed in the bank (my customer's site) while the alternate computer was installed in my data center, several kilometres away. While the systems passed all its internal diagnostics, the main computer could not automatically transmit live data to the alternate computer. Without the storage of live data in the alternative computer, the systems were useless as a "hot site". After desperately trying for a week, my team could not get the systems to transmit the live data across. I decided to call the German engineer for help.

Luck was not with me. The German engineer was on long vacation, leaving me, the impatient customer and the million dollar system that refused to work. How could we get the systems to work? We began from the basics. We analyzed the circuits, reconfigured the systems, checked the hardware and software a hundred times, and wrote a couple of micro-instruction codes, but still it did not work. By then we knew the entire systems like the palm of our hands. Finally, we decided to trace the signals with an oscilloscope. We found that the main computer did transit the data, but it stopped at the input leg of an integrated circuit, and did not come out of the output leg. What was that integrated circuit chip supposed to do? No one knew.

I was a young man then – wild, idealistic, and dangerous. I reckoned that since no one knew what that integrated circuit chip was supposed to do, and that it was a show-stopper, our team decided to by-pass it. So we cut out the chip from the circuit board and soldered a wire across its path. Our by-pass worked. Data transmission started streaming out from the bank's main computer, through several kilometers of cables across to a different part of the city into our data center's alternative computer. The customer was overjoyed. I grinned, as happy as a gynaecologist who had just delivered his first baby.

Champagne, flowers, and congratulation cards poured in. We had a press release and were featured prominently in the back page of the Straits Times[12] , Singapore's main newspaper, as the first electronic vaulting in Asia. No one knew about our makeshift wire bypass, our little

---

[12] Straits Times,(1993, 03 31). Electronic Vaulting Service. Safe as a Bank? , p. SS4.

microprograms, and the missing chip on the brand new million-dollar systems.

THE POWER OF BELIEF

A few days later, my phone rang. "Remember me?" said someone with a German accent. It was the German engineer who had gone on leave! He congratulated me and we chatted for a while. Before I hung up, he asked a question that astonished me: "John, how did you get the systems to work?"

How did I what? He explained that although he'd designed the electronic vaulting concept and systems, he was unsure if it would work. He admitted that when he sent me the hardware and software configurations, he thought I wanted to set it up for my internal use. He realized much later after the systems were sold to a customer. It turned out that our systems were the First Electronic Vaulting System in the WORLD.

I learned an important lesson that day. My team did not realize that the systems never worked. At the back of our minds, we assumed (and firmly believed) that it worked in Germany. Therefore, the only problem we needed to figure out was "How to get the systems to work".

In contrast, our German friend who designed the concept and systems was unsure if it would work. When one is unsure, half the brain says yes while the other half says maybe.

The lesson I learned was:

"If you believe you can, you are right. If you believe you cannot, you are also right."

Henry Ford

Powerful Quotes

DEFINING YOUR EVEREST

Summiting Mt. Everest is a mountaineer's dream. It is the vertical tip of the Earth and the ultimate challenge for hundreds of climbers who toil every year to reach its peak. For every few who succeeded, hundreds failed and many died.

Mt. Everest may be too far and too cold for most of us non-climbers. But while Mt. Everest sits so far in solitude waiting for those who have the courage and determination to summit it, there is another Everest deep inside each of us waiting for us to take the first step, to muster up the courage, and to conquer it.

Deep within you and me, each of us reading this book or walking down the hustle and bustle of the streets, there is an Everest. Each and every person has a dream, be it big or small. There is something we have always wanted to do, to venture into, and somewhere we have always wanted to go, and something somebody always wanted to be. But these dreams remain within us for years, largely because these dreams were usually too big, too absurd, or cost too much. Over the years, we learned that dreams were meant for those who slept. Dreams disappeared when one woke up.

So what is an Everest?

An Everest is that something you always wanted to DO, to HAVE, or to BE. Like Mt. Everest, it is a goal that is almost impossible to achieve, unless you are willing to take the risk, put in preparation and time, be persistent, and develop alternatives and contingencies.

Perhaps that is why a dream remains a dream. Perhaps it's too cold, too far, or too difficult. Perhaps these are just some of the many mild excuses for us to remain within our comfort zones.

Each of us defines our Everest differently. To an injured person confined to a wheel chair, being able to walk is the Everest. It takes courage, strength, and months of sheer determination to just place one leg in front of the other. It may take many more months to walk on his own; and years to be able to run like a normal person again. To that individual, that is his Everest.

To one child, getting a distinction in his examination is an Everest, yet to another, a chance to go to school can be his Everest. To one man, owning a Porsche is his Everest, yet to another, passing his driving test is his Everest.

To a corporate executive, achieving a 15% business growth next year while it was growing at a traditional rate of 8% per annum may be his Everest. To another executive, he will not rest until he hits the 50% growth every year. To an organization, maintaining itself on the top 10 most admired companies is its Everest; to another corporation, being number one is the Everest. During the economic crisis, surviving another day in business itself was an Everest.

An 80-year-old man I met in the park laughed when I explained my concept of Everest to him. He said, "Waking up tomorrow is my Everest!"

So what is YOUR Everest? It is personal and is defined by you. But it must be something really big, something that you always wanted to achieve and something that you are willing to take risks and make sacrifices for. Your Everest can be as grand as your life-long ambition or can be as short as your last New Year's resolution. Whatever it is, it must be a quantum leap from today's state, a cliff over your competitors, or a gigantic step away from your norm.

Incremental growth, edging over your competitors, winning by a whisker, maintaining your current top position, etc, are not considered an Everest. These are things that you have been doing well, and although it has proven results, it is merely the next mountain, not an Everest.

So what IS and what IS NOT an Everest?

IS	IS NOT
Exponential Growth	Linear Growth
Overtaking the market leader	Winning the next nearest competitor
Running a marathon	Running a kilometer further
Making it to the President's Club	Exceeding your sales quota by 10%

As you can see, an Everest is when there is a breakthrough in the way you think, the targets that you set, the things you do, and the end results that you have achieved.

WHY EVEREST?

Knowing the difficulties that the mountaineers face during the Mt. Everest summit bid, have you ever wondered why there are still people who want to climb Mt. Everest each year?

Have you pondered...?

▶ What motivates these mountaineers to spend several years of their youth training for the climb?

▶ Why would they risk their life and limbs to go there knowing that there is danger regardless how of much preparation they make?

▶ What makes these people leave behind their families to pursue such a thankless task?

▶ What rewards will they get when they reach the peak?

For all those great sacrifices and risks, we would think that the reward must be valuable. The reality is that there is no pot of gold, no pretty angels, or magnificent dragons up there. There are only heaps of snow, harsh cold temperature, piercing wind, some remains of past tragedies, a few little tokens, and prayer flags left behind by conquerors. It is not easy to comprehend why the mountaineers would undertake such personal risks and effort to achieve the Mt. Everest dream. Perhaps it is simply ego, perhaps it is self-esteem, or perhaps it is me versus the world. Whatever it is, these heroes have set their minds to achieve it, and they succeeded.

The simplest answer to WHY is WHY NOT?

If others can do it, WHY NOT ME?

If I want to do it, WHY NOT NOW?

The "WHY NOT" attitude lets you see potential opportunities that are waiting to happen. Once this mindset is activated, it's hard to turn it off. You start seeing potential solutions everywhere.

SUMMARY

Summary Notes

1. The power of the mindset drives people to greatness.

2. Think, Believe, Dream, Dare – Disney

3. Document your dreams, define your Everest
    a. Stretch yourself; define your goals greater than your abilities.
    b. Commit to a goal greater than your norm.

4. Conquer your fears, one small step at a time
    a. What's stopping you?
    b. What's the worst that can happen?
    c. What are the benefits if you succeed?

5. An innovative mindset propels the rest of your innovation journey.

    Believe that you can. Do something great. Take massive actions.

6. Start today!

CHAPTER 4
TEAMING FOR
INNOVATION

"Explain to me again how this thing can
help us move faster."

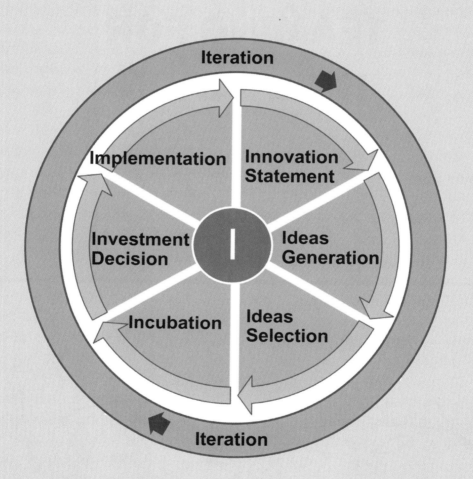

CHAPTER 4: TEAMING FOR INNOVATION

At a precise timing, the S.W.A.T. team sprung into action. Nobody needed to wait for the command from the team leader. They had already agreed to strike at midnight, and had synchronized their watches to the second. The snipers squeezed their triggers in unison. Crack! The deadly rounds pierced through the air and hit the chief and his right hand man in their heads. Blood splattered across the room.

Sensing their cover had been blown, the remaining terrorists reached out for their weapons. Window panes shattered as stun grenades that were lobbed in exploded. Shocked and immobilized, the terrorists could not react at all when the S.W.A.T. team rushed in to finish them off one by one.

High above the roof, another team had earlier rappelled down the helicopters and pre-inserted themselves into position. Swiftly, they swung themselves through the top floor windows. Machines gun fire rattled and bullets ripped through the cool night air followed by eerie screams and tumbling bodies. Then silence.

As suddenly as it had began, the drama was over. Hostages were rescued unharmed. The sun rose to greet another mission accomplished. Another headline.

Isn't this the hallmark of excellent teamwork?

What does it take for us to train a team like this?

This book is written for both an individual innovator and for organizations. If you are an individual innovator, you may skip this chapter. If you are innovating for an organization, this chapter will help you define the different roles for your innovation team. Your organization may be a local enterprise or a multi-national corporation; this chapter aims to explain how individuals can work together as teams and how teams can work together to align their innovations to the corporate vision.

Like the SWAT team, an innovation team needs to work together to accomplish the mission with the maximum impact and minimum resources. Each innovation team member needs to be trained with the proper skills set and mindset. For teams to succeed there must be:

► Resources
► Capabilities

RESOURCES

Thomas Edison said, "To invent, you need a good imagination and a pile of junk."

Powerful Quotes

We shall discuss about developing and enhancing good imagination throughout this book, but you still need a pile of junk for the team to play with, to experiment, and to prototype. This book is probably the first piece of "junk" that serves as the instruction manual about what to do with the other pieces of "junk".

The Innovation Owner's role is to ensure that all the resources (hardware, software, infrastructure, working space, money, etc) are available for the team, including the budget to purchase the pile of experimental junk. Of course, if the budget is limited, we can always beg, borrow, or steal the junk. Thomas Edison and his team did a lot of cannibalization, meaning they re-used parts from previous prototypes and other machines to create new machines.

Next, you need a workplace for your experiment, models, and prototype. The workplace can be a bench or a laboratory. It can also be a market place or a selected shop or a selected customer (also known as a guinea pig) to prototype and test your creations.

To save time and effort, I encourage multiple prototypes and concurrent market trials. One of my clients wanted to launch a new innovative service, but they were unsure of the price points and service option offerings to package. Working with them, we launched six different service packages in six different shops in six different geographies at the same time. After two weeks of selling, we picked the top two best-selling service offerings and re-launched them, this time, in all the six shops for another two weeks. The final top-selling service package became the one we officially launched to several hundred shops across the whole country. It was a resounding success.

In this case, our budget was the working capital to launch six different prototypes and our workbench was the six shops. You can consider this as an experiment where one product worked excellently well while the other five prototypes were thrown back into the pile of junk.

In a different case, I had a client (a government agency) who did not have a pile of junk or a budget for the team to play with. During one of the brainstorming sessions, the team agreed to purchase a device from the internet as a prototype. As the government procurement process was cumbersome, it took the team many months and many management meetings to approve the purchase (which could be easily paid for with a credit card). By then, the team was several months behind schedule.

CAPABILITIES

I define **Capabilities** as the ability to use the **Resources** to convert ideas into innovations. Capabilities include, but are not limited to:

► People (with roles and responsibilities defined)
► Skills sets, expertise, knowledge
► Processes

In brief, the innovation team for an organization comprises of the following team members:

► Innovation Owner
► Facilitator
► Innovation Team
► Sponsor
► Innovation Administrator

Let's see what their roles and responsibilities are.

INNOVATION OWNER

Who owns the Innovation Statements? In the next chapter, we shall craft out the Innovation Statements and describe this in further detail.

Whose career is at stake if this innovation swims or sinks?

Who will be the hero to reap the fruits if the innovation project is successful?

A simple short answer is that this individual is the stakeholder. He has an issue to fix or a dream to be fulfilled and needs the innovation team to achieve it with him. He provides the background information and related data so that the team understands the current situation. He defines what and where the future will be if the innovation succeeds.

Take an example of a Sales Director who is accountable for bringing in sales revenue for the organization. He is measured by the sales quota and he prospers when the sales revenue exceeds his quota. He is the best person to be the Innovation Owner for sales and revenue related innovations.

In another example, a Regional Business Manager is accountable for the profit and loss of a mobile communication business in the countries under his charge. He has sales, marketing, logistics, administrative, and operational people reporting to him. He should be the overall Innovation Owner for all innovation projects in the mobile communication business in those countries.

The Innovation Owner is usually a manager or director who is accountable for a specific business or a department. He must have decision making authority and have direct access to senior management (sponsor).

The Innovation Owner has the following responsibilities:

▶ Define the Innovation statement and objectives (where are we going?)
▶ Furnish the team with the background information (where are we now?)
▶ Present to a sponsor the budget and necessary resources
▶ Define and document the commitments in terms of the objectives, measures, milestones, and rewards for the team (if applicable)
▶ Ensure the project and progress meets the objectives outlined in the Innovation Statement.
▶ Making the investment decision or selling to sponsor to obtain the go-ahead decision

FACILITATOR

A facilitator is an individual who helps the innovation owner to:

► Clarify and understand the Innovation Statement and its objectives
► Explain the rules of brainstorming to the team
► Conduct the brainstorming session during the Idea Generation phrase
► Draw the knowledge and ideas out of the team
► Keep the group intact, on-track, and on-time in their discussions
► Help the team reach an acceptable and sustainable solution

He or she is contently neutral and does not take sides or express his/her personal opinion during a discussion. He is not part of the process, but is the controller of the process. In an organization, a facilitator can be the Innovation Owner, or the Innovation Team leader, or a team leader from another team or simply anyone who is trained to facilitate a brainstorming session.

A fun way to look at his job is that the facilitator is neither the father nor the mother of the baby, but he helps to deliver the baby. You can deduce that the Innovation Owner owns the baby.

INNOVATION PROJECT TEAM

These are the heroes in the SWAT team. They make innovations happen and they create tomorrow's newspaper headlines. Like the SWAT team, we need different types of professional expertise (like the sniper, the signaler, and the detonation expert) and skill sets (like rappelling, lobbing a grenade, and shooting straight). This team plans the mission, navigates through obstacles, and accomplishes the mission (without sacrificing the hostages). Remember, tomorrow's headlines will be different if the hostages die.

The team should comprise of:

► The Innovation Project Manager, who is also known as the Team Leader. His main roles are:
  ■ To lead the team and to make sure they are on track, on time, and on budget

  ■ Be the central point of contact between the team, the Innovation Owner, and the management

  ■ Can request for resources and escalate issues to the Sponsor or Innovation Owner where necessary

  ■ Can be appointed by the Innovation Owner or nominated by the team themselves

  ■ Accountable to lead the team to achieve all of the project goals and objectives while within the project constraints. Typical constraints are scope, time, and budget.

► Staff from stakeholder departments
  ■ It is vital that the team must have some members from the stakeholder department, i.e. customer service innovation project must have staff from customer service department

  ■ These staff will represent the stakeholder department in articulating the issues, collecting data of current status, presenting data, getting resources from the stakeholder department, conducting trials, gathering feedback, and interfacing with stakeholder end-users, etc

► Cross-functional staff

   ■ It is vital that each innovation team should have a number of staff from different functions (administration, finance, engineering, sales, marketing, operations, R & D, legal, etc)

   ■ Members see the issues and ideas from different perspectives as they are not "buried" in the issues themselves.

   ■ They can also adopt a naïve approach and question the most obvious fundamentals and assumptions that were taken for granted by the members within the stakeholder's department.

► Subject matter experts

   ■ These are people with some area of expertise that is critical for the success of the innovation project. E.g. if you are working on an environmental green project, then you need a green expert to advice and help you. If you are looking into health issues, then having a nurse or a doctor in your team is essential.

   ■ These experts can be internal or cross-functional. Often, they could be invited or engaged from external organization.

   ■ Their contribution is to furnish the team with technical specialized knowledge that is critical for the project to progress

SPONSOR

You should be able to spot this guy from a mile away. He walks around with a fat wallet leaving a trail of dollar bills behind. He breaths money, talks money, and smells like money.

The sponsor's main role is, you guess it, to sponsor the innovation project. In the SWAT team analogy, he's the guy that buys you the helicopter and weaponries. It's no big deal if you save the hostages but crash the helicopter. It's a big deal if the helicopter is unscratched, but the hostages die.

Sponsors can be your CEO, the Chief Innovation Officer (CIO), board of directors or your senior vice-president. They can also be venture capitalists or business angels. Their primary objective is to invest money to make more money.

To get them to sponsor you, you need to sell your innovative ideas and convince them to part with their money. Note that for high risk projects, there is a fine line between sponsors and suckers. Your job is to make sure they are not the latter.

INNOVATION ADMINISTRATOR

This is a unique role that I created for an organization-wide innovation program, which I codename the Everest Challenge. The program consists of several innovation projects, each headed by an Innovation Owner. The CEO or CIO, who will be the main sponsor, and sets the Innovative Vision for the entire company. Given a timeframe of 12, 18, or 24 months, the various innovation teams raced to reach the Everest Summit (where their missions are accomplished). Frequently, there will be rewards for the team or individuals when they reached the Summit.

The Innovation Administrator's roles (in such a comprehensive organizational-wide innovation program) are:

- ▶ To keep track of the progress of all the innovation teams
- ▶ Generate status updates and reports
- ▶ Update the management and sponsors of the progress of individual teams throughout the journey
- ▶ Compute the savings or earnings achieved by the innovation projects
- ▶ Compute the rewards for each team (if applicable)

An Innovation Administrator is only needed if the organization is running multiple concurrent innovation projects at the same time.

With the team in place, now is the time for action.

The Innovation Team:

Innovation Statement: _____

Innovation Owner: _____

Team Leader: _____

Team Members: _____
                      _____
                      _____

Sponsor: _____

Innovation Admin: _____

Resources: _____
                      _____
                      _____

Budget: _____

Timeline: _____

Actions:

	When	Who
1)		
2)		
3)		
4)		

CHAPTER 5
INNOVATION
STATEMENT

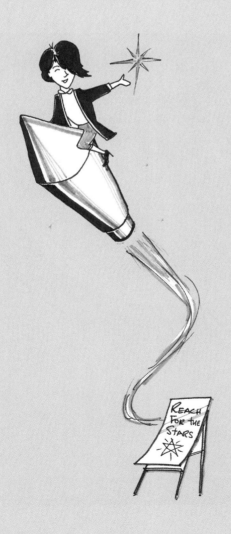

REACH
FOR THE
STARS

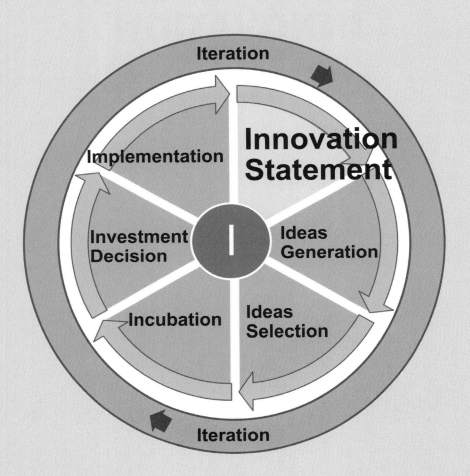

CHAPTER 5: INNOVATION STATEMENT

Every great business begins with a grand vision. Every great invention begins with a dream.

Innovation and creativity should neither be based on random flashes of thoughts nor sporadic sparks of inspiration. Unlike popular beliefs, most companies do not hire a team of innovators to look at the ceiling the whole day long. I had spent many days staring at ceilings, but the only things that moved were the ants and the spiders. Innovative companies form innovation teams, develop structure ways to systematically churn out thousands of ideas, sort out ideas, and select ideas with the most potential.

Where do you begin your search for innovation?

Three sources of innovation:

- ▶ Inefficiency and Ineffectiveness (Problem)
- ▶ Inspiration (Dream)
- ▶ Inadequacy (Not Enough)

INEFFICIENCY AND INEFFECTIVENESS (PROBLEM AREA)

This is the most common source of innovation. Watch out for areas of inefficiency and ineffectiveness in your workplace. Look out for problems within your company.

Have you been frustrated by inefficiency or ineffectiveness before? I am sure you have. Instead of grumbling about it, stop and think. Is this problem widespread? Is it costing the company a lot of money, delays, or wastage of resources? If so, these are great areas of focus for your innovation.

There are two great advantages of starting your innovation effort with a problem:

1. You are likely to get plenty of support from your boss and peers. All of them want to get rid of the same problem too. You can form teams with the various stakeholders who may benefit from the innovative resolution of the problem.

2. It is easier for you to justify resources and funding. How much funding? That depends on how big is the problem. The funding can usually be recovered from the savings resulting from the removal of the problem. So start with the most frustrating and resource wasting problem first.

How does innovative problem solving defer from the traditional problem solving?

In traditional problem solving, we investigate the problem, collect data, analyze data, find the root cause, and find possible solutions to the problem. The final solution for traditional problem solving usually restores the situation/system back to the normal status again.

On the other hand, in innovative problem solving, the final solution may be totally different from its original status. In innovative problem solving we explore creative ways like rearranging the steps, reverse the problem, eliminate some steps, or even eliminate the entire process.

INSPIRATION (DREAMS)

The second powerful source of innovation is through inspiration and dreams. While using a problem as the basis of innovation is easier to gain acceptance, few great earth-shattering inventions are ever created based on problem statements alone. Dreams and inspirations, on the other hand, can result in life-changing revolutionary innovations. They are naturally much more difficult to conceive, to sell, and to implement.

Difficult to conceive

This is due to our logical thinking brain that rejects all irrational ideas. In a nanosecond, our brains will flush such illogical ideas down the toilet bowl without pausing to ask "how can this be possible?" A common natural mistake is that we tend to judge our ideas and brand it as impractical before the ideas can even be fully conceptualized. Because of our natural tendency to judge ideas, most of our creative ideas are dead before they are born. We end up with lots of practical normal ideas.

Difficult to sell

Nobody will believe you. Your boss and colleagues will laugh at you. Your family will advise you to stick to your day job. You need money and resources to conjure the proof of concept but you will find difficulty in finding sponsor to believe you. No proof of concept means no funding. It is the chicken and egg situation where neither can proceed without the other.

How many times have we heard our colleagues and our bosses telling us ...?
- ▶ "It wouldn't work"
- ▶ "We have tried that before"
- ▶ "Where do we get money to fund an absurd project like that?"
- ▶ "What if it fails?"

More often we are not even able to sell to ourselves. Our brain says "no" before the great idea can see the light of the day. These are all negative thoughts – thoughts that kill ideas. I called them Idea Killers.

To get rid of Idea Killers, we simply replace them with Idea Growers. Idea Growers focus on positive thoughts and explore how such ideas can be groomed, exploited, or made possible. By simply adding a "How to" in front of a Problem Statement, we can convert the "problem" into a solution-focused innovation statement.

Examples of Idea Growers:

▶ Instead of saying "It won't work", try saying:

  ■ "How can we make this idea work?"

  ■ "Let's try to brainstorm how this concept can be applied to our industry."

  ■ "How can we prototype this idea to get the proof of concept?"

▶ Instead of saying "we do not have the budget", try saying:

  ■ "In what ways can we do this innovation within the existing budget?"

  ■ "How can the project be self-funding?"

I like to share a powerful quotation:

Powerful Quotes

"Some men see things as they are and ask why.

Others dream things that never were and ask why not."

George Bernard Shaw

INADEQUACY (NOT ENOUGH)

While many people understand the first two sources of innovation, few understand what inadequacy is. It is simply a force of not being happy with the current performance or the accepted industry performance.

I was delivering an innovation workshop at the Excelsior Hotel in Hong Kong. To illustrate what inadequacy means, I called my workshop participants to gather by the conference room window overlooking Causeway Bay. "How's the traffic along Victoria Park Road today?" I asked.

Most of my participants remarked that the traffic is okay. "What is okay?" I probed.

"There's no jam," one participant said.

"This is normal traffic," commented another, "about 30 km/hr."

"Nothing wrong with it," pondered the third.

"If your brain accepts the situation as normal, then nothing creative can be conceived. Why can't the cars be travelling at 60 or 80 km/hr in the middle of Causeway Bay?" I challenged the participants.

"Oh no! There will be a lot of accidents," one participant instantaneously blurted out.

I smiled, "Then our Innovation Statement can be – How to enable traffic to travel at 80 km/hr without accident?" Suddenly the class understood. Seeing beyond today's accepted norm is what inadequacy is about.

I met a CEO in Malaysia in an industry conference several years ago. During the break, I explained to him how I had helped my clients use innovation to generate lots of ideas that can help their companies grow.

"I don't need that," he snorted arrogantly. "We are already growing; in fact we are leading the market."

I congratulated him and probed how much was his growth rate. "10%" he remarked proudly, "the rest of the market is growing at only 8%."
My next question stunned (or angered) him: "Why aren't you growing at 20%?"

"Impossible!" he replied and rattled off a long series of "professional insights" about how his industry behaved, about the low profit margin, about the tight market situation, and went on to give me his 10,000 supporting reasons why it was impossible to grow beyond his world record of 10%.

I waited patiently for him to finish and to put a forkful of noodles into his mouth. "Your brain is suffering for 'Contented Inadequacy'," I remarked. Immediately his jaws dropped. "If your brain tells you that 10% is enough, then it is enough. If your brain tells you that beyond 10% is impossible, then it is impossible," I explained, noticing a drop of gravy dripping onto his tie.

From the three sources of innovation (inefficiency, inspiration, or inadequacy), you have identified an innovation project that you want to embark on. You must next encapsulate it into an Innovation Statement.

CRAFTING AN INNOVATION STATEMENT

The Innovation Statement is a statement that clearly defines what the team or the business unit wants to achieve using innovation within a time frame. It defines the goal and the destination. It serves as a beacon for the innovation project and keeps everyone on track.

There are several ways to express an Innovation Statement:

1. As a goal, an objective or a set of objectives for the team
2. As part of an annual planning exercise, where the innovation statement needs to be realized by the end of the financial year. For example:

    1) To achieve $x million in sales revenue in Financial Year 20xx
    2) To achieve cost savings of $Y million through innovation
    3) To shorten the Z process time from three days to one day

3. As a vision for the company, the division, the business unit or the team. This corporate-wide innovation statement can be divided into mega-projects for the various business units, which in turn form teams to tackle their respective innovation projects. I shall discuss more about how such a grand vision can be fulfilled through multiple teams across the enterprise in later chapters.

What is the difference between an Innovation Statement and the normal business objective or a normal corporate vision?

Many business and management books[13] describe a popular acroym, SMART, which define the five elements that should be contained in a good business objective:

Specific, Measureable, Achievable, Relevant, Time-bound

One of the biggest mistakes is for the innovation team to use SMART to measure their innovation project. As a result, their innovation can churn out only ordinary results that are "achievable" and "relevant".

An Innovation Statement need not necessarily be SMART. It defers from the normal business objective in many ways. Let's examine what and where the differences are.

---

[13] Drucker, P. F. (1954). The Practice of Management.

▶ Specific

Traditional business books state that the objective should be concrete, detailed, and well defined. It is results-focused and action-orientated.

In innovation, you may be specific in an Innovation Statement. But one danger of being too specific is that it restricts your idea generation process. Specific Innovation Statements may render you too restrictive in your scope of possible ideas.

I recommend that your Innovation Statement can be broad initially then fine-tuned to be more specific at a later stage.

▶ Measurable

Traditional business books state that the outcome should be tangible and we should be able to measure it. If possible, we should be able to capture the measurement automatically using existing systems or processes in tangible format. This thinking leads to the notion that if you cannot measure something, then that something cannot be your objective.

Some innovations can be measured, especially in the arena of improvement in operational efficiency, problems resolution, increase in revenue, etc. Internal measures like return on investments and time-to-market remain valid.

But how can you measure an innovation that has not been created yet? For a brand new innovation, traditional external measurements like market-share disappears. There is no such market and definitely no competitor. There may not be any existing measures. When you innovate and create a brand new product, you create a brand new world.

As an example, if you invent television, how do you measure market share when you are the only one in the market? Technically, how do you measure the whiteness and blackness of your black and white TV? If you cannot, then how do you tell your customers that your TV looks better?

Moving on, you invent the color TV. How do you measure hue and color? How can you tell your customers that your TV is more brilliant and more colorful than your competitors?

Moving on again, assuming your TV now has the scent capability. How do you measure smell? How can you compare that your TV's scent is more precise than the competitors?

As part of the innovation, you need to invent the measurements as well.

▶ Achievable

Traditional business books state that targets should be realistic and attainable under normal circumstances. The rationale is that if an objective is not achievable or realistic, the team will not be motivated to achieve it. They know that they are going to fail anyway.

In the arena of innovation, the reverse is true. Any innovation that seems achievable from the beginning is usually a modification or any adaptation from existing products or services. New products with such minor innovations or enhancements compete in the same market and may command a premium price for only a short period before competitors "copy" the enhancement.

True innovation and breakthrough technologies often appear to be initially impossible.

Was going to the moon possible before Apollo 11?

Was cloning possible before Dolly?

Instead of focusing on what is achievable, great breakthrough thinkers focus on their inspirations and dreams. Whatever seems impossible initially can be overcome with the various techniques taught in this book.

▶ Relevant

Traditional business books state that objectives should be relevant to the team or business unit. The team has the responsibility and authority to influence the outcome and to drive actions to achieve the objectives.

Relevancy of Innovation Statements is important to the innovation team as well. Irrelevant projects that are unaligned with business and corporate objectives are usually flushed down the corporate toilet at a snap of the fingers, as none of the business managers will sponsor it.

History has countless irrelevant ideas that were thrown out of the window, picked up by passionate innovators, funded by venture capitalists, after which they grew into multi-million-dollar new businesses.

I have two recommendations here:

- Corporate executives must evaluate the innovative ideas from the perspective of "what could be possible in the future world" instead of "what is relevant to my business now"

- Idea-originators do not forego their dreams even though no one wants to sponsor them. Keep your dreams alive, be persistent, be passionate, be patient. The angel will appear.

► Time-bound

Traditional business books state that a fixed time frame should be stated and agreed. Usually, time frame targets are aligned to the business financial and planning time frame or fiscal year.

In innovation, however, time is not so deterministic. The idea generation stage and the innovation research and development stage cannot be determined upfront. These stages are iterative. It means these stages may recur if the initial set of ideas does not solve the problems at hand.

Through practice and experience, innovators can generate thousands of ideas within minutes and filter out the suitable ideas to select the best ideas within the same day. Such techniques will be covered over the next few chapters.

As part of the good innovation project, the team should strive to accomplish the project in a much shorter timeframe than the norm, with minimal resources and risks.

AN AWESOME INNOVATION STATEMENT

On May 25, 1961, John F Kennedy inspired the world with his audacious goal "to land a man on the moon before the end of the decade." While the world was inspired, many scientists in NASA were shocked. They did not know how to land a man on the moon! They did not even know how to drop a peanut onto the moon. But the U.S. President had set a goal and had even defined a timeline before the NASA scientists could figure out the how to. The mission was earth-shattering, the problems encountered were insurmountable.

That audacious Innovation Statement set the engine running. Budgets were approved, expertise and resources were built. Projects that were aligned to the moon mission were endorsed. Other non-moon missions were canned or thrown out of the window. Everybody was working on one and only one goal. Thousands of problems surfaced; millions of possible ideas and solutions were explored and sorted.

By and by, the dream became a reality. On 21 July 1969, Neil Armstrong became the first human to set foot on the moon, where he announced, "One small step for a man, one giant leap for mankind." Millions of people on Earth were awed at the unforgettable grainy images of astronauts planting the U.S. flag on the moon.

Moon landing was a far-fetched fantasy in 1961. What if President John F Kennedy had set a realistic achievable objective?

In the arena of innovation, if S.M.A.R.T. is not totally valid for the definition of an Innovation Statement, then how can we set our objectives? How can we define our Innovation Statements?

John F Kennedy's Moon Mission Statement carried a lot of elements that made up an awesome Innovation Statement. It is:

▶ Inspirational
   ▪ It touched the hearts and minds of people around the world

▶ Memorable
   ▪ People remembered his Moon Innovation Statement many years after he had said it

▶ Granny-proof
   ▪ Everyone understood the moon statement clearly. Kennedy's mission was not only understood by the NASA rocket scientist; it was clearly understood by everyone, from the taxi drivers in New York to the pizza-delivery man in Chicago.

   ▪ It is important that a great Innovation Statement should be granny-proof because if a grandmother can understand it, then a Senior Vice-President can understand it.

LEARNING STEPS

Learning Steps

INNOVATION STATEMENT SELF-CHECK

Create the first draft of your Innovation Statement. This can be for yourself, your team, or your organization.

Check:

▶ Is it inspirational? Do you think the statement will motivate you and your team to change the world?

▶ Is it memorable? Tell your spouse. Tell three more friends. Do they remember it the next day or next week?

▶ Is it granny-proof? Do your spouse and friends outside your industry understand it fully? If you have to take the time to explain the Innovation Statement to them, then it is not granny-proof enough.

Examples of awesome, memorable, granny-proof Innovation Statements:

▶ A PC on every desk (Steve Jobs)
▶ A Coke at an arms' reach
▶ Happiest Place on Earth (Disneyland)
▶ Greatest Service Center in the World (Hewlett Packard South East Asia)
▶ One call, One solution, One smile (Hewlett Packard Global Solution Center)

HOW HIGH IS YOUR EVEREST?

If "A" for "Achievable" (as in S.M.A.R.T. objective) is not valid, then

► How high or unrealistic should we set our objectives for innovation?

► Will teams be de-motivated by the unachievable targets?

We know that Mt Everest is 8848 meters (29,029 feet)[14] , but how high is YOUR EVEREST in your heart?

Every Everest climber dreams of summiting the mountain. Standing on top of Everest, the climbers touched the heavens. At the summit, climbers and dreamers felt only the angels above them and the rest of the world beneath their feet. For that dream, they dedicated years of their life training hard for it. Through incredible risks and effort, they conquered the peak.

Mount Everest has a definite height; climbers either reach it or they don't.

What about YOUR EVEREST?

How high is YOUR EVEREST?

How high should it be?

It depends on the following:

► Who you are and what your dreams are?

► How ambitious you are and how much energy and determination you like to commit?

---

[14] A MacGillivray Freeman Flim (1996). Everest (IMAX) [Motion Picture].

► How hot is your burning passion?

The height of YOUR Everest is YOURS to determine. It must excite your heart and fascinate your mind.

Well, just fixed a height! Your own inspirational height. It can be extremely high or marginally high. It must be proportional to the amount of passion and hard work you are prepared to invest.

You need not compare your Everest with the person next to you. To a new entrepreneur, earning his first million is an Everest; to another, repaying his debt is the Everest. To one strong and healthy man, completing a marathon is an Everest; to another who is injured, learning to walk again is an Everest.

I challenged my workshop participants to set their Everest goals beyond what they had achieved in the past. In a corporation, Innovation Statements containing Everest Goals are best set from top executives down. For example: the CEO with his board members, the Managing Director with his management team, the business manager with his reports, etc. The Everest Goals can be divided into sub-goals and propagated down the organizational hierarchy.

If the team traditionally grew at 10%, then let's break the tradition and go for 20% growth next year! If your market or industry grew at 10%, can you double or triple the industry trend? If we are number three in the market, let's aim to be number one next year. Aim to be inspirational rather than achievable.

But what if it is not achievable? We never grew beyond 10% before. We are always number three in the market. How can we suddenly be number one next year? If you do not aim for the moon, you will not reach the sky. Do expect objections and resistance from your team at this stage (See Chapter on Innovation Mindset).

The answers to all these objections are that:

Powerful Quotes

We achieved what had achieved for all these years because we had been thinking and doing the same thing the same way all these years. We were thinking and doing things linearly and traditionally, not innovatively

Over the next few chapters, we shall learn and be equipped with:

▶ The ability to generate thousands of new ideas within minutes on how to overcome problems or search for solutions,
▶ Discover the new-found skills create new innovations and
▶ Proven techniques to achieve breakthrough results.

We, therefore, should be:

Key Point

- **Thinking innovatively instead of thinking traditionally**

- **Working and thinking in parallel instead of in sequentially**

- **Growing exponentially instead of linearly**

- **Quantum leaping instead of edging pass our competitors**

FORMULATING AN AWESOME INNOVATION STATEMENT

All notable inventions and innovations in the world are remembered forever.

Do you want to be remembered forever?

If you want to invest 6 or 12 or 24 months on an innovative project, it makes sense to do something worthwhile, something notable and/or something memorable. In another words, if you can change the world, you may as well do it.

Where do you start?

Learning Steps

LEARNING STEPS

You start with the most impactful, the most important and the most urgent problem to solve!

Look into your organization, can you find it?

Let's say you want to initiate a cost saving project.

Look into your financial statement to find the portion of the business that takes up the biggest chunk of your expenses. That's your first and most impactful starting point. Let's assume that your highest expenses come from logistics. Your next logical step is to zoom in to investigate your highest cost item within logistics and try to eliminate it.

Similarly, if you want to grow and sky-rocket your revenue, you need to find out the portion of your business with the greatest potential that can fetch you the most revenue. Innovate on those:

- Products with the greatest potential
- Major clients that need your product most
- Market segment that you contribute most to (or depends most on your products)
- New market with the greatest potential, ...

In summary, your project should not be routine or reactive.

To be awesome, focus all your energy on what matters most.

Two simple Innovation Statements:

1. To save $1 million in logistics spare parts
2. To grow $10 million in revenue for Product Z

Or your statements can be more specific:

1. To save $1 million in logistics spare parts by shortening the value chain within the next 12 months
2. To grow $10 million in revenue for Product Z through a new e-marketing channel

Key Point

- **Innovation statements can be set generally first, then fine-tuned to add the specifics later.**

REFRAMING THE INNOVATION STATEMENT

As the Innovation Statement defines your destination, it is extremely important to define it correctly before you embark on your journey. Throughout my years with innovators and inventor wannabes, I had met many teams who did double or triple U-turns in the midst of their projects. After several intensive months, these teams had to begin from square-one again as they found themselves heading the wrong way. All these U-turns sap out precious energy, time and resources, which you need to propel your project forward.

Caution!

Before you begin the next Idea Generation phase, I highly recommend that you spend some time with your team to rethink, refocus, and reframe your Innovation Statements.

It's easier and cheaper to do double U-turns on your Innovation Statements then to a U-turn in the midst of your innovation journey.

Take a simple example. Assume I have a mice infestation problem in my factory. Mice are running all over, eating my grain, biting through my sacks and my electrical wirings, soiling my products and scaring away my customers. My current mouse traps do not work effectively.

LEARNING STEPS

Learning Steps

My first draft Innovation Statement will naturally be:

1)   How to build a better mouse trap?

If we generate ideas with (1), we will get lots of different ways to design mousetraps, different types of mousetraps, different ways to trap mice, etc.

Take some time to reexamine the above statement and see if you can refocus and reframe it in multiple ways. The purpose is to explore different perspectives to make sure that we are comfortable with the original statement or if perhaps there are better ways of phrasing it, different ways of wording it, or different angles to approach the problem.

Examples of reframing the above mousetrap statement:

2)   How to **<u>get rid of</u>** the mice?

Comparing this with Statement (1), this statement is broader. We are able to generate more ideas that are not "trap-related". We can think of different ways to kill mice (e.g. smoke them out from their holes, poison them or drown them)

3) How to **<u>prevent</u>** mice from coming in?

This statement does not involve killing, just preventing.   If we can seal up our office, factory and home, then we do not need to care about the mice in the outside world.

4) How to **deter** the mice from coming in?
By substituting one word from (3) PREVENT with DETER, we get a totally different Innovation Statement with a whole lot of different innovative ideas. DETER ideas are more effective than PREVENT as mice will not dare come in even if they have a chance to.

5) What **opportunities** can I generate with mice?
This is remarkable! Since we have lots of mice in our factory, what opportunities can we create with them? How can we make money from them? Hmmm, think of a brand new industry of tasty, nutritious, barbequed mice. What about mice-skin handbags and belts? Or send them to the zoo as animal feeds…

As illustrated, the above five different ways of phrasing your innovation statements will drive your project teams in different directions. Imagine embarking on the project with the first innovation statement, and you would have missed out all the opportunities.

The solution to Statement (4) could be putting a tiger in your factory and Statement (5) reverses it to send all the mice to the same tiger in the zoo. Imagine the disaster if you had implemented Statement (2) and poisoned all the mice before realizing that your local zoo is willing to offer a price for your mice.

Which Innovation Statement works best for you?

Can you think of a few more ways to paraphrase your Innovation Statements?

SUMMARY

Summary Notes

1) Three sources of innovation:
   i.   Inefficiency (problems)
   ii. Inspiration (dreams)
   iii. Inadequacy (not enough)

2) Turn Idea Killers into Idea Growers.

3) Be careful with you set S.M.A.R.T. objectives; examine it from the innovation perspectives.

4) An awesome Innovation Statement should be:
   i.   Inspirational
   ii. Memorable
   iii. Granny-proof

5) Start your innovation project with the most impactful, most urgent, most important problem area or growth area.

6) Three steps to craft your Innovation Statement

   i.   Write the Innovation Statements.
   ii. Re-frame your Innovation Statements.
   iii. Brainstorm the various Innovation Statements. Discuss with your team before you embark on your Innovation Journey.

CHAPTER 6
IDEAS
GENERATION

"But Doctor, we are running out of ideas."

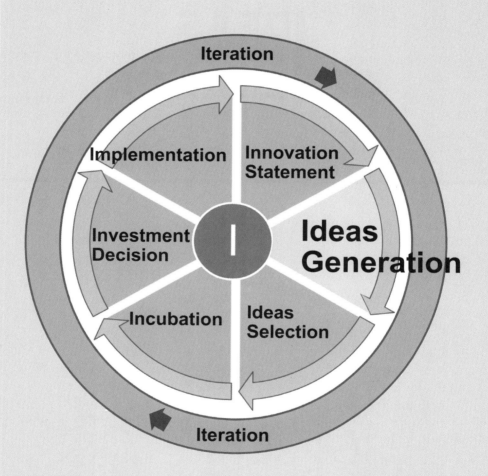

CHAPTER 6: IDEAS GENERATION

Powerful Quotes

"If you walk into a zoo and see penguins and tigers, you are not thinking.

However, if you see the tuxedoes in penguins and apply it to the world of fashion,

and the camouflage patterns in the tigers and apply it to the world of military strategy,

then you are thinking innovatively."

John Seah

CLIMBING EVEREST THE EASIER WAY

Having defined your Innovation Statement, you have defined where to go. Naturally the next question is, "How to go there?"

In innovation, we don't just want to get there. We want to get there in the shortest possible path, in the shortest possible time with the least amount of resources. We want to be there ahead of our competitors. We want to be the first to reach our peak. Conquering Everest with ropes and ladders is far too difficult for me; I want something better, faster, and easier.

In 2003, I met an Everest climber during a seminar. I was there to deliver the morning talk on innovation while he was there to motivate and to share his Everest experience with the participants. While exchanging name cards, he noticed that my company is called Everest Innovation. Curious, he asked if I climbed Mt. Everest.

I replied, "Of course!"

"Which year?" he asked.

"Every year," I replied.

He was surprised. The Everest community was extremely small, he wondered why he had not heard of me if I had indeed climbed Everest every year. I explained that while he climbed Everest the hard way, using ropes and ladders, I climbed the Everest the smart way, using innovation. My Everest, as well as my clients' Everest, was located in our minds and in our hearts.

We discussed the various ways of reaching the summit of Everest without climbing. I listed ideas like:

► Parachuting off from an airplane,
► Landing a helicopter on Everest …

Before I could continue, the Everest climber interrupted me by saying that no one could land a helicopter on Everest. "The air up there is so thin that the helicopter blades have nothing to bite on," he said knowledgeably.

I challenged him that through innovation, nothing is impossible. We can:

► Build a more powerful engine
► Double the number of helicopter rotor blades
► Increase the surface areas of the blades, etc.

I was right. Two years after our conversation, on May 14th, 2005, an Ecureuil/ AStar AS350B3 piloted by the Eurocopter X-test pilot Didier Delsalle[15] , landed at 8,850 meters (29,035 feet) on the top of Mount Everest.

This tremendous achievement broke the World Record for the highest altitude landing and take-off ever, which set an ultimate milestone in the history of aviation. After taking off from its base camp Lukla, Didier Delsalle landed his Ecureuil the top of Mount Everest. As required by the FAI - International Aeronautical Federation, the aircraft remained on ground more than two minutes on the top of the world before flying back to Lukla. [16]

The next day, Didier flew and landed his craft again just to make sure that the attempt was repeatable.

Stepping out of his helicopter, Didier Delsalle commented: "To reach this mythical summit definitively seemed to be a dream; despite the obvious difficulties of the target to be reached, the aircraft demonstrated its capability to cope with the situation."

His solo flight broke the record for highest helicopter landing, previously held by Nepalese Lt. Col. Madan Khatri Chhetri, who in 1996 rescued climbers Beck Weathers and Makulu Gau near Camp I at approximately 6,096 meters (20,000 feet).

This feat has opened a new world. It has important implications:

▶ Everest tourism is now possible (subjected to Nepalese authority approval)
▶ High altitude rescue is now possible. Before this flight, climbers facing difficulties within the Death Zone (beyond 8000 meters) were doomed to die as no one could rescue them at such high attitudes.

---

[15] http://www.mounteverest.net/news.php?id=1327

[16] http://www.eurocopter.ca/asp/cmNews050524.asp

Many of us are like my Everest climber friend. We are blinded by our industry knowledge of what IS-NOT possible. Because our brain shuts out what IS-NOT possible, we are not looking at ways that ARE possible.

I was amazed to find out that the Ecureuil AS350B3 helicopter that landed on Everest was unmodified. This means that it could land on the Everest summit anytime. Then why did the world think that landing a helicopter on top of Everest was not possible? It was because no one had attempted that height before. Remember that the highest attempt was by Lt. Col. Madan. He had difficulty landing and taking off from Camp 1. There was a documentary film entitled "Everest", a MacGillivray Freeman production[17] for the IMAX theatres, which showed Col. Madan risking his life in a dramatic rescue, struggling to take off at 6096 meters (20,000 feet) . In the film, we also learned that a previous similar attempt resulted in a crash. From that day, the world had established it as a fact that "the air was so thin that the helicopter's blades had nothing to bite on".

Facts are double-edge weapons. The great strength of knowing facts is that, once established, we no longer need to question facts; we simply make our decision based on them. However, that is also its greatest weakness – we no longer question facts.

No one questioned or noticed that Col. Madan was piloting a crabby old Nepalese helicopter. It was not the latest or greatest. It's like attempting to set a world speed record with an old Ford car. And the world accepted it as a fact.

Now that we have found an easier way to reach the summit of Mount Everest, we can also find an easier, cheaper, and faster way to land a helicopter on YOUR Everest.

---

[17] A MacGillivray Freeman Flim (1996). Everest (IMAX) [Motion Picture]

YOUR BEST IDEAS

Everyone has his opportunities to get the best ideas and to be the most creative. I asked my workshop participants:

- ▶ During what kind of activities and situations do you get your best ideas?
- ▶ When do you get your best ideas?

Some responses we received were:

- ▶ 'When I am faced with a problem'
- ▶ 'When there is a deadline'
- ▶ 'When I am pressurized'

Interestingly enough, another group of responses we had observed were in the opposite situation:

- ▶ 'When I was about to sleep'
- ▶ 'Late at night'
- ▶ 'First thing in the morning'
- ▶ 'After a movie', 'During a movie'
- ▶ 'When I am taking a shower', 'jogging', …
- ▶ 'When I am eating', 'toileting', etc.

These show that while necessity may be the mother of invention, a playful and relaxed mood and environment are also fundamental to creative thinking. Most of us get great ideas when we are in a relaxed mode. This is because we are more willing to try something new and different when in a lighter mood, when our defenses are down and when we are not so concerned with rules and practicality. This is the time when your logical brain is not computing and your creative brain begins to play. So if you want creative ideas, relax. Take a break, stroll around the garden, smell some roses, watch the children play or simply watch a movie. Even during office hours.

Thomas Edison came out nearly every morning while in Fort Myers and sat at the end of the dock, which stretched out into the bay, holding a fishing pole, dangling it in the water. However, he never had any bait on the hook. Thomas Edison confessed that "I fish with no bait because no one bothers me, neither fish nor man." Thomas Edison was actually fishing for ideas out in the river. Creativity can be found at the end of the fishing pole, if first of all, your line is in the water, and you never stop searching.

Archimedes was relaxing in his bath when he found his Archimedes principle!

Similarly, Issac Newton discovered gravity when he was relaxing under an apple tree. He did not discover gravity in his laboratory. He probably worked hard on his formulas for months, and then suddenly it all makes perfect sense when he was relaxing beneath the apple tree.

BRAINSTORMING IDEAS – THE TRADITIONAL WAY

After crafting a perfect Innovation Statement, the next step is to generate lots of ideas on how to attain the goals outlined by the Innovation Statement. This is the brainstorming stage. I asked many of my workshop participants how they would normally conduct their brainstorming session. Most of them replied that they would appoint a facilitator who would write the brainstorming topic on the whiteboard or flipchart and ask for ideas from the project team. As the team contributed their ideas, the facilitator would record the ideas on the whiteboard for discussion.

I asked the participants how many ideas they would normally generate in a half hour brainstorming session. Their replies ranged from 10 to 20. This number was far too low. It was highly unlikely and unrealistic to expect one outstanding idea from a pool of 20. Another disadvantage of traditional brainstorming was that only practical ideas emerged. This was because, in front of colleagues and managers, few creative and seemingly unpractical ideas would appear.

This traditional brainstorming technique was pioneered by Alex Osborne in 1941. While it is a good technique for soliciting random and different ideas from the team, it has two weaknesses:

1. The brainstorming participants think serially. When one person contributes an idea, the rest listen. This method is extremely slow and unproductive as it encourages a "one brain thinks at a time" syndrome.

2. Anyone who disagrees with the idea tends to speak out and the team dives prematurely into discussing the said idea. Ideas are killed even before they are raised. Participants may have ideas, but feel that their ideas could be too simple, too expensive, too crazy, etc. They fear criticism from their friends and therefore such ideas are not even raised and recorded.

Both these weaknesses arise because ideas are judged for their merit before they are recorded. To overcome this weakness, it is important to separate the Ideas Generation Phase from the Ideas Selection Phase. It is like drinking and driving. If you drink, don't drive. If you drive, don't drink. Ideas generation and ideas selection are two distinct phases that do not mix.

SPAWNING IDEAS

Chicken lays eggs.

Fishes and frogs spawn.

If frogs lay eggs, they would have been wiped out from the surface of the Earth millions of years ago. To ensure survival of their species, frogs spawn by the thousands. Hopefully, a few of their strong (and lucky) offspring can survive predator attacks and grow into adulthood to carry on their family line.

Similarly, to reach the Everest summit faster, safer and cheaper, we need lots and lots of ideas to select from. Not mere 20, not 50, and not even a hundred ideas. Several hundred ideas would be nice. A thousand would be superb.

But how do you generate (or spawn) a thousand ideas within half hour?

LEARNING STEPS

PRINCIPLES OF GENERATING IDEAS

Learning Steps

When generating ideas, I look for the two important principles:

Volume
- ▶ **The Principle of Volume states that the higher the volume, the more chances we have to find a diamond from the mountain of ideas.**
- ▶ As Linus Pauling (chemist and Nobel Prize winner) said, "The best way to get a good idea is to get lots of ideas." If the brilliant IDEA you are searching for is not recorded in the pile, then how can we expect to find it?

Uniqueness
- ▶ **The Principle of Uniqueness states that the more unique your idea is, the lower chance your competitors have thought of it and the higher chance for you to lead the world.**

- ▶ When generating ideas, it is important to create out-of-the-box ideas. Go for something weird, something wild, something crazy, or something out of the blue. Think of something borrowed from a different industry, something adapted from a book you have read, or a science-fiction idea from Hollywood. Be as unique as possible.

▶ At the Ideas Generation Phase, it does not matter if the idea is practical or not. We shall figure out the practicality of selected ideas during the Incubation Phase. Figuring out the practicality of ideas will stop and kill creative ideas before they have the chance to see sunlight.

CONCURRENT THINKING

Concurrent thinking is a technique to get your team to think and focus on same Innovation Statement at the same time, but churn out multiple ideas concurrently. Concurrent thinking is not a new idea. The Information Technology (IT) folks invented parallel processing way back in the 1960s. In the quest to drive the computer processing unit (CPU) to run faster, the IT engineers connected several CPUs together to run the programming instructions concurrently.   Parallel processing minimizes the idle time of any CPUs. Any CPU that had completed its tasks picks up its next task from the master queue. In this way, no time or resources are wasted. This approach is also known as multitasking.

Our human brain does parallel processing too. The brain simultaneously processes millions of instructions to interpret the incoming light signals from the eyes, converts them into images, processes the images to make sense of them (in terms of color, motion, form and depth), then issues "action instructions" as a response to what the brain sees.

While the brain is busy processing the "sight" function, it concurrently handles the breathing function, the beating of the heart, the balancing on the feet, and the detection of a mosquito that has just landed on the left toe.

If one brain can do a million things concurrently, why should we put 20 brains in a room to think serially?

IDEAS GENERATION TECHNIQUES

There are hundreds of idea generation techniques. I shall introduce to you the following techniques that I love best because they are simple to learn and extremely efficient.

- ▶ Silent Brainstorming
- ▶ Scamper

SILENT BRAINSTORMING

In contrast from the traditional brainstorming, which is extremely noisy and distractive, Silent Brainstorming does not encourage talking or discussion. The principle is to separate the process of thinking (generating ideas) from the process of discussing if the ideas are good or bad (judging).

Material needed:
- A box of memo pads

You can buy these memo pads from any stationery shop. Their sizes range from 80mm x 80mm to 100mm by 100mm (normally available in boxes of 500 to 1000 sheets). I prefer the loose individual sheets over the bound pads. Some people use 3M pads, but I do not encourage them for two reasons:

- ▶ They are sticky. A feature that is annoying and a hindrance when you are sorting out thousands of independent ideas.

▶ They are costly (3M will hate me for this), especially when you are going to use thousands of sheets.

LEARNING STEPS

Learning Steps

Here's how it is done:

1. The facilitator writes the Innovation Statement on a whiteboard, or flashes them on the projector screen.

2. Either the facilitator or the Innovation Owner may explain the background situation and Innovation Statement to the team and clarify any doubts or technical terms before the brainstorming starts.

3. The Facilitator explains the rules of the session:
    a. No talking, just thinking and writing.
    b. Write each idea on a separate memo sheet. Always begin a new idea on a fresh memo sheet. This is important as sorting is based on individual ideas on independent sheets.
    c. Leave a 20 mm gap from the top of the memo sheet. This 20 mm space will be used later during sorting.
    d. When generating ideas, ensure that each idea carries enough words to be useful. As a guideline, five or more words can carry an idea effectively across. For example:
        i. "Cut cost" by itself is useless

ii. "Cut cost through minimizing material wastage" is more useful.

4. The Facilitator starts the clock and allows about 7-10 minutes for this session.

5. Beyond the seventh minute, the facilitator will notice that ideas are running dry and participants are struggling to generate the next set of idea with ease. At this stage, the facilitator can ask everyone to place their ideas in the center of the table or pass it to the person on their right. Participants can read their friends ideas to trigger another set of fresh ideas. Write all new ideas on fresh memo sheets.

6. Allow another five minutes for more ideas to be generated. Stop when the team runs out of ideas. Let the clock tick on if the team is still scribbling ideas.

Because everyone jots down their ideas silently, we do not disturb each others' train of thought. Each participant is free to write their thoughts anonymously without fear of being ridiculed by their peers. Ideas should flow like water from a running tap. No disturbance, no judging, and no worries about peers or management's opinion. Creative ideas, no matter how wild and crazy, can then flow without constraint. This is the power of silent brainstorming.

If each participant generates one idea a minute, then a team of 10 can easily generate a hundred ideas every 10 minutes. This is the power of concurrent thinking.

There is, however, one disadvantage with this method of silent brainstorming. Because great minds think alike (or fools seldom differ), there is a tendency that many of the ideas generated may be duplicated. This is not a big problem as we can throw out such duplicates later during our Ideas Selection Phase.

SCAMPER

SCAMPER is a brainstorming method that was first developed by Bob Eberly[18] , and is used widely by a lot of innovators in the market. Michael Michalko[19] developed it further in his book *Thinkertoys*. I found SCAMPER or (SSCAMPERR) extremely effective in drawing out tons of ideas efficiently.

LEARNING STEPS

Learning Steps

SCAMPER stands for:

S – Substitute – components, materials, people, or roles

S – Simplify – simplify processes, the number of steps

C– Combine – mix, combine with other features, parts or services

A– Adapt – alter, change function, or apply into a different environment, geography, or market segment

M – Modify – increase or reduce in scale, change shape,modify attributes (e.g. colour, form, format, features)

P – Put to another use – in a different way, not what it was originally designed for

E – Eliminate – remove elements, simplify or reduce to core functionality

R – Reverse – turn inside out or upside down or start from the last step

R – Rearrange – rearranging priorities or the different steps in a process

---

18 Eberle, Bob. (1997). SCAMPER: Creative Games and Activities for Imagination Development. Prufrock Press .

19 Michalko, Michael. (2006). Thinkertoys: A handbook of creative thinking techniques (2nd Edition). Ten Speed Press.

We can use each of these words as a trigger to generate innovation questions or ideas.

Let's start!

S – SUBSTITUTE

I love substitutes. It's the simplest way to generate lots of fantastic ideas. Take the Innovation Statement, substitute a word here and a word there; we get a lot of new ideas with the substituted words and new phrases. Besides substituting words, we can substitute material, people, roles, etc, into the Innovation Statement to create more different ideas. Look at the list of ideas you have generated for the problem you are trying to resolve or goal you are attempting to achieve. Are you able to substitute any words to change it to a different or better idea?

SUBSTITUTE WORDS

Example: I need $1M to buy a house. How to GET $1M?
Substituting Words: How to SAVE $1M?
                     How to EARN $1M?
                     How to BORROW $1M?
                     How to STEAL $1M?

You get what I mean. By merely substituting one word, we change the whole Innovation Statement and all the ideas and action plans.

SUBSTITUTE ROLES

Do we always have to sell through sales professionals in our company? Try substituting (or complementing) your company's sales force and sell through channels or partners. Why not substitute them with a web portal? We can also devise schemes to sell through our employees or customers.

Why not do them all!

As part of the rehabilitation effort for inmates, the Singapore Prison Service invested a lot of time and effort in providing inmates with education and training. Such training for thousands of inmates costs money. Prison officers brought this Innovation Statement into my workshop:

How to save money in inmates' training?

Using "Substitute", we generated the following ideas:

1. External trainers and teachers train inmates
2. Officers train inmates
3. Inmates train inmates
4. Inmates train officers
5. Inmates train public

Statement 1 was the current situation that cost a lot of money.
Statement 2 was out because officers had much more specialized duties to perform.
Statement 3 was the best as there are multiple benefits:

a. There is a lot of talent within the inmate community (including a handful of MBAs and PhDs)
b. Give the talented inmates some meaningful jobs to do
c. Help the trainer-inmates gain good merit points that earn them early release.
d. And, of course, save lots of money as these talents are already inside the prison

In Statement 4, substitution reverses the roles. Officers can learn from the inmates to understand their needs better and to better prevent potential convicts from committing crimes. Learning from the inmates, officers can develop better programs to help them reintegrate back to society.

In Statement 5, inmates are in the best position to share their experience in awareness programs and educate the public about how to deter potential convicts and to better combat crimes.

The keyword 'Substitution' triggered a lot of exciting action plans and programs for this batch of participants. Many of these action plans were later approved by their management and implemented. The participants achieved their objectives and saved lots of money for the prison services.

SUBSTITUTE MATERIAL

The first laser printer designed for use with an individual computer was released with the Xerox Star 8010[20] in 1981. Although it was innovative, the Star was an expensive ($17,000) system that was purchased by only a relatively small number of businesses and institutions. After personal computers became more widespread, the first laser printer intended for a mass market was the HP LaserJet 8ppm, released in 1984, using a Canon engine controlled by HP software.

With Canon controlling the vital component in their biggest printer business, HP was at the mercy of their competitor. It severely affected HP's competitiveness, profitability, and perhaps, long-term survival. It was a critical problem HP needed to fix desperately.

HP had a long tradition of having coffee-breaks at 10:30 a.m. Besides taking a mental and biological break from work, the HP coffee-breaks served as an important time of the day where managers and staff caught up with each other on a personal basis, getting to know new employees, chatting about families, hobbies, inspirations, issues, and of course, the weather. During one of these traditional HP coffee breaks, an HP R&D engineer noticed coffee dripping from a coffee machine.

---

[20] http://en.wikipedia.org/wiki/Laser_printer

It gave him an exciting idea ⇨ Substitute coffee with ink.

If each of these black coffee droplets could be shrunk to the size of a pixel and spurted onto the paper at a precise timing, then each droplet of ink could form one black dot on paper. Synchronized dots formed characters and words.

What did he invent?

The HP Deskjet printer that conquered the world.

S – SIMPLIFY

What can you simplify? How to simplify?

Which areas in your company to simplify?

Simplification is very useful for process-related innovation.   I used simplification a lot, especially for cost reduction and time saving projects.

LEARNING STEPS

Learning Steps

Here are a few suggestions:

1) Processes
   a) Which processes in your company are too complex, too cumbersome, and too time-consuming?

2) Rules
   a) Are there rules that are outdated?

b) Which rules are confusing and need simplification?

3) Shortcuts
a) Where are the short cuts? Actively look out for them.
b) Are there more efficient bypasses?
c) Will a simple workaround suffice in place of a full solution?

4) Number of steps
a) Too many? Can we reduce them?
b) Is every step necessary?
c) What if I reduce one of the steps, will the process still work?
d) How can I make the processes work, without that step?

5) Reduce the number of people involved
a) Do I need so many people?
b) Can I simplify each of their tasks?
c) Can I combine their roles?
d) Can I get rid of some of the non-critical activities?

6) Reduce the number of decisions
a) How many decisions are involved in this process /activities?
b) Are they really necessary?
c) Can I pre-approve some of the non-critical decisions to hasten the process?

7) Reduce the number of choices
a) Are these choices or options necessary?
b) Do they serve a critical demand or are they just good-to-have?

Watch out for clues from employees or customers who hate to fill up a complex form or struggle in understanding a process or have problems explaining something to a client. Look into the complaint letters or employee suggestions. All these are symptoms that lead you to the targeted areas where you can begin your simplification innovations.

Do your processes include steps that can be automated? When looking for candidates for automation, look for processes that are time-consuming, routine, and repeatable. Take a New-Hire Process for example. A new hire walks into your office one day.

▶ Does he have a personal computer (PC) ready, installed with the required software with user accounts created for him?

▶ Is he ready to work from Day 1 or has he got to fill up more forms and wait a couple more days while the documentations are being processed and approved?

▶ Since we expect the New Hire Process to be repeated frequently, we can watch out for any delays, process gaps, and breakdowns, and then automate them to smoothen out the process.

Are there decision points that are automated? Note that for every decision point that a manager has to make in a process, there is an inbox and outbox. This means a one-day delay for the manager to read, make a decision, and send out his approval. Mathematically, a process with three decision points will take an average of three days to process.

Interview the various managers involved.

▶ Do they really need to make those decisions?

▶ Or do they just need to be informed?

▶ How many such requests have they approved versus disapproved?

▶ Under what circumstances would they disapprove?

Document the findings. You will find that a high percentage of the routine requests are approved automatically. Highlight the exceptions and automate the rest.

Are you providing too many product options for your clients?

Which options are popular and which rarely matter?

If you offer a choice of six color options (or feature options) for your products now, how much revenue would you lose if you reduce it to four options, compared with how much logistics and manufacturing costs you would save?

In many cases, the company will be much more profitable by getting rid of the bottom two least popular options (which few customers buy anyway).

Over time, many organizations add more and more options to a product (or a service) in the quest to get more customers and to cover more market segments. Too often, we forget to retire the unprofitable products and services from our offerings. Simplification is a good platform to reexamine our offerings and make it real friendly and simple for our customers to choose.

You may be quick to remark that Simplification is not very innovative.

I agree.

However, the results may be an industry breakthrough.

If you can automate and reduce a three-day process turnaround time to three seconds, will you be the fastest in your industry?

How much more value-add or revenue can you create when you offer a three-second turnaround time while all your competitors still have the legacy three-day turnaround time?

If each of your six product options cost the same amount to manufacture and to warehouse, then by simplifying your offerings from six to four you may save 33%. Balancing that with your loss of, say 5% from customers who wanted those two least popular options, you will still make a lot more profit. A simple project like this can save you millions of dollars.

C – COMBINE

Look at the list of ideas you have generated from previous methods.

▶ Which ideas can you combine or build upon each other to create another idea? Something different and better.

▶ Are there different products or features you can combine to cut costs?

▶ Are there paperwork or forms you can combine for better efficiency?

Organizations like Hewlett Packard and Lexmark noticed that their customers were having the problem of too many machines cluttering up their office desks. First, there was the computer, with its keyboard, mouse, and monitor. Then the user added a printer. Soon, their desks would be cluttered with a fax, a scanner, and a copier. The last thing a user needed was to add another desk as he ran out of space to work.

What would you invent?

The All-In-One printer or multi-function printer (MFP)[21] is a machine that combines the functions of printer, copier, fax, and scanner. In the early stages of product development, these were separate products. The designers and marketers studied the market, understood the customers'

---

[21] http://en.wikipedia.org/wiki/All-in-one

problems, and discovered a need for a combination of the four products into one to reduce the "footprint" on the desk.   The scanner and copier shared the same input imaging technology.   The printer, the fax, and the copier shared the same printing output technology. Combining them into an All-In-One made a lot of sense from the users' and marketers' perspectives as all the technologies were already available.

Microsoft bundled its products Powerpoint, Word, and Excel to create an Office Suite, which provided purchasing efficiency for the customers while achieving ease of sales and more revenue for Microsoft.

A car drives on the road and a boat propels in sea. Ever dream of combining them?

Hollywood had, in a James Bond movie. Gibbs Aquada[22] invented a car that looks like a sports car and runs like a sports car. However, when it runs out of road and splashes into the sea, just press a button, and in 12 seconds flat, its wheels tuck gracefully under its body. You are now boating, not driving. The Aquada cruises at a cool 100 m.p.h. on the road and 30 m.p.h. afloat, powered by a proprietary jet-propulsion system that generates nearly a ton of thrust. The Aquada was highlighted by TIMES magazine[23] as one of the coolest inventions for the year 2003.

What about combining roles?

HP sold PCs with or without installation services. In the mid-1990s, when a customer bought a PC with installation service, HP sent the PC to the customer (via a courier service, costing $30), and separately, an installation technician (via an outsourced agency, costing $60). During a brainstorming session, the management looked into the possibility of combining these two roles. A decision was made to train the courier

[22] http://www.gibbstech.co.uk/aquada.php

[23] TIME. (2003). Coolest Invention of the Year 2003. http://www.time.com/time/2003/inventions/invaquada.html .

drivers on how to perform the installation service, backed by a helpdesk hotline should they run into technical difficulty. This new combination of roles benefited all parties in four ways:

1) The drivers and courier company earned more money ($45 up from $30)
2) HP saved money ($45 down from $90)
3) Technicians were freed to do more value-added technical work
4) Customers got their PC installed faster. There was no longer need to wait for two persons.

In today's converging technologies, the information community had combined voice, data, and multimedia into mobile phones. Adding in cameras, music, and videocam functions into mobile phones was a piece of cake. Then they linked the mobile phone to the internet for greater power. What other functions can you combine into a mobile phone? Perhaps one day, your mobile phone can make you a cup of coffee.

Impossible, some of my participants said.

Why not?

Because it would be absurd for anyone to put coffee powder and hot water into the mobile phone?

I challenged them to focus on "How can?" instead of "What is existing". Focus on the possibilities instead of the difficulties. Within a few seconds, one of the participants said, "Using the mobile phone, we can dial a number which is linked to a coffee vending machine near you. Money will be paid through your telephone company."

Another participant said, "Let's put a smart chip into the mobile phone and a scanner on the coffee vending machine. Your mobile phone can become an e-wallet."

Through innovation, if your mobile phone can make you a cup of coffee, what else is not possible?

One day, in the near future, a businessman noticed a teenager floating a meter above the ground. Intrigued, he asked the teenager, "You are levitating in mid-air, how did you do that?" The teenager shrugged his shoulders and remarked, "I don't know, my mobile phone did it!" Perhaps some day in the near future.

A - ADAPT

To adapt is to find ways to use or sell the existing products or services:

- ► In another industry
- ► For a different purpose
- ► In another market segment
- ► To different clientele
- ► In a different geography, etc

Take an existing product (or service). Will something that does not work in one industry work for you? Can you adapt this product to a different environment, use it in a different situation, or to fulfill a different set of needs? If you can, you have just found gold. Well, maybe, found another revenue stream.

Adapt from another industry

Do you have a pressing problem or issue that is affecting your entire industry?

Look out for best practices in a different industry. Will something that works in another industry or company work for you, your company, or your industry? As an example, the Six Sigma and LEAN manufacturing framework and methodologies were first developed for the manufacturing industry. They have now been adopted and used by professionals across many other industries like telecommunications, banking, insurance, transportation, logistics, consumer retails, etc.

In the budget airline industry, fast turnaround time (time taken to clean the cabins, refresh, reload their supplies, disembark and board their passengers) is extremely critical. An aircraft in the parking bay equals huge investments idling away, depreciating by the minutes. If the airline can keep the aircraft in the air by finding ways to shorten their turnaround time, they can make one more flight per day, generating more revenue for the company.

Who is the expert in fast turnaround time?

Who should they learn from?

Watch and learn from the Formula One folks! The F1 team can jack up the car, loosen the nuts, remove the old set of tires, replace new set of tires, tighten all the nuts, pump in the fuel, lower the jack, and send the car back to the race within eight seconds.

Duck Tours[24] offers tourists a unique and fun experience by providing them with both a city land tour and a river cruise. Tourists can find these cute yellow duckie-shaped amphibious vehicles in cities like Singapore, Boston, Miami, Washington, London, etc.

The idea was adapted from the military. During the early days of World War II, the allies were faced with a tough tactical problem: How could they unload cargo and men from their ships in places where the dock facilities had been destroyed or simply did not exist? The answer was to unload cargo directly over the beach. But how? They needed a vehicle that was half boat and half truck that could run on land and water. Code-named DUKW, the first "DUCK" was actually a GMC (General Motors) truck enclosed in a water-tight shell.

---

[24] http://www.ducktours.com.sg/ducktours.html

The SARS story

In March 2003, the world nearly came to an end when the Severe Acute Respiratory Syndrome (SARS)[25] virus spread around the world. Within a matter of days, SARS spread from the Guangdong province of China to rapidly infect thousands of individuals in Hong Kong, Singapore, and Canada at a deathly speed of a Jumbo 747. Within weeks, 8096 individuals in some 37 countries around the world were infected. Almost overnight, people were collapsing and dying. Nurses and doctors who attended the infected got infected themselves.

To stop the spread of SARS, there was a desparate need to isolate the infected from the uninfected especially in crowded places. As fever was the only known symptom for SARS and the virus was airborne, we needed to find an efficient way to screen large groups of people for fever. This was especially critical at immigration checkpoints and airports to control the cross-border spread of SARS. However, the conventional means of taking temperature using ear and oral thermometers were too slow and inconvenienced everyone.

Chuck Hampton, a Nokia Project Manager working in Singapore[26] , had an idea to use thermal scanners to screen people with fever. He had seen such thermal imaging cameras used in the Nokia facility in San Diego. California, to scan overheated electronics.

On 2nd April 2003, he wrote an email to the Singapore Health Minister, Lim Hng Kiang. The Ministry of Health quickly approached the Defence Science & Technology Agency of Singapore to evaluate, and if possible, implement the solution.

---

[25] World Health Organization. (2006). SARS: How a global epidemic was stopped. WHO Press.

[26] Ministry of Information Communication and the Arts, Singapore. (2004). A Defining Moment: How Singapore beat SARS. Singapore: Stamford Press Pte Ltd.

The DSTA[27] sprung into action and came up with a design concept using the Singapore Armed Forces' military thermal imager. Singapore Technologies (ST) Electronics, which designs and manufactures thermal imagers, was roped in to work together in this project. The idea was quickly turned into a prototype within a week.

The result was the Infrared Fever Screening System (IFSS), a system that could screen large groups of people quickly, non-intrusively, and with a high level of confidence in sieving out febrile persons. It was the first thermal-imager-based system in the world to be used solely for mass human temperature screening. On April 11th, this new invention was deployed at the Singapore's immigration checkpoints, airports, hospitals, and major government buildings. Quickly, the invention caught the world's interest and soon the IFSS systems could be found in numerous airports, hotels, and hospitals around the world.

This was an excellent case where technologies used in the military were adapted to civilian usage in a matter of a week, thus saving the world and avoiding a deadly pandemic. The IFSS was voted as one of the best TIMES' Coolest Invention of the Year 2003[28].

Adapt to another market segment

The world of computers, electronic, and consumer products changes at a supersonic rate. New products are being rolled out from manufacturing lines every day, only to be made obsolete by their competitors' more powerful blockbusters the very next day. Product R&D is expensive and companies are struggling with ever shortening product life cycles. How can such companies survive and continue to roll out greater and better products quickly and at minimal costs?

---

[27] DSTA. (2005). Development & Deployment of Infrared Fever Screening Systems by Tan Yang How and Team. https://www.dsta.gov.sg/index.php/DSTA-2005-Chapter-1/ .

[28] TIME. (2003). Coolest Invention 2003. http://www.time.com/time/2003/inventions/invfever.html .

One great idea many companies in these industries employ is to adapt their products to another market segment in order to renew their product lifecycles. Let's say a company has a great Product X for their high-end customers, Product Y for their mid-range customers, and a low cost Product Z for their low-end customers. When the company announces and releases their latest Product W to replace Product X for their high-end customers, they can repackage Product X as a new Product X1 (by changing their external plastic covers) for their mid-range customers. Similarly, Product Y can be repackaged into Product Y1 for the low-end customers.

By adapting to different market segments, each product enjoys multiple life cycles. The end of life for one market segment can be the beginning of life for another lower market segment. The bulk of the R&D cost can be recovered and the company simply invests in the re-designing of plastic covers, colors, minor repositioning of buttons, etc.

M - MODIFY

The questions you can ask yourself are:

▶ What features in my worst (or best) selling products can I modify to turn them into winners?
▶ Which part of the process can I modify to make it more efficient?
▶ How can I modify my proposal to make it a breakthrough?

You can also ask "what if" questions:

▶ What if I modify the length of this piece of equipment to …?
▶ What if I modify the feature of this product to include an extra button for …?
▶ What if I modify the screen to make it so flexible that …?

Contrabands are items that the prison inmates should not possess, like a penknife smuggled in by a visitor, a metal fork from the dining hall, a razor shaver stolen from the hygiene kit, or an innocent nail carelessly thrown away by a contractor. A vengeful inmate can turn such contrabands into a lethal weapon in times of a gang fight. Inmates who possess such weapons illegally would take great care in hiding them in cracks and corners where the officers cannot see or detect.

As part of their routine duties, officers in the prison services need to search for contrabands in their premises and from their inmates. This task, though important, is laborious, boring, and time-consuming. Every day, prison officers need to climb ladders to peek at odd high corners above the cabinets and doorways, crawl under the tables and beds to see if anything is taped below, and dive into the toilet cisterns to retrieve concealed contrabands.

During a brainstorming session, the officers generated a lot of ideas using the keyword "Modify". What can we modify to do our job more effectively? They stumbled upon an idea to modify the length of the video camera handle.

By taping a video camera onto a long pole, officers can have a good view of high places, low corners, hard-to-reach crevasses without the need to climb (and carry) ladders or to crawl into low places. Using the zoom features, they can see small objects at greater distances. This simple modified camera-on-a-pole increased their efficiency by more than 30%.

Modify Services

While products are manufactured in a factory far away from the consumers or customers, services are produced during and as part of their interactions with the service providers and customers. Because of the malleable nature of services, they are much easier to modify to suit the customers' needs. Once a product is being manufactured or built, it is very costly to do any modification. Imagine the customer trying to move the on-off switch from the top to the side of the product while it is being built. The entire manufacturing plant needs to be reconfigured and new moulds need to be built.

Products can be modified if it is a deliberate business strategy. Examples include:

1) DELL sells computers via their website with lots of options (central processor speed, memory size, hard disk size, network options, etc) that customers can choose from.

2) IKEA and many home-improvement companies offer do-it-yourself furniture options for you to mix-and-match to suit your own needs.

Questions to ponder:

▶ What can you modify to suit your customers' diversified needs?
▶ Which products? Which features?
▶ How to enable modifications to be done cheaply and efficiently?

Services can be easily modified any time. In fact, services can be modified on-the-fly. This means that while the service provider is performing the service, the customer can make minor modifications at the same time. Examples include a tailor fitting a suit for a customer, a hairdresser working on a hairdo for a bride. This process is commonly known as customization. Some companies provide customization (or modification) free of charge, while others charge a fee for the value added.

Learning Steps

LEARNING STEPS

We should therefore take advantage of the malleable nature of services. Think for a moment and explore how you can generate more revenue by creating and providing your customers with a lot of modifiable options:

1) Core services (main service that you provide)
   a) Observe your customers. Observe your service agents delivering their services to the customers. If necessary, conduct a survey.

      i) Which features do your customers retain (because they like them)?

      ii) Which features do they modify most (because they dislike them)?

      iii) What other requests do your customers make that we can deliver (thus creating new value)?

      vi) What other requests do your customers make that we cannot deliver (leading to the development of new services or products)?

   b) Compile the frequency of such modification requests.

   c) Analyze and evaluate if you need to:
      i) Retain your Core Service features or
      ii) Modify them based on your observations or
      iii) Spin them off as new chargeable service options.

2) Service Options
   a) These are complementing services that customers can pick and choose depending on their needs, desires, and budget.

Example: A computer is sold with a one-year warranty. An extension to a three-year warranty is an option customers can add.

   b) Brainstorm all possible options for service upgrades.

Examples: A computer is ..." align with the start of examples below
   i) Extending the service (e.g. 24 hours by seven days support versus office hours only support)
   ii) Providing a faster service (e.g. a VIP priority queue)
   iii) Providing more convenient (e.g. on-site repair at your home versus return-to-store repair)
   iv) Bundling more services (e.g. buy Service A and B, Service C comes free)

P - PUT TO OTHER USE

Every product (or service) is engineered for a certain purpose. Faced with a problem, can we take a product and put it:

▶ To other use?
▶ For other purposes?

Mountain climbers often have to navigate deep crevasses when they climb mountains or cross glaciers. Crevasses are deep cracks in thick ice. It is so deep that it is impossible or impractical to climb down and up across the other side. As a quick bypass, climbers tie ladders together and use them as temporary bridges to cross the crevasses. Ladders, which are designed for a user to climb to a higher place, are "put to other use" as a make-shift bridge for the climbers.

Most telecommunication companies charge their customers for the talk-time used. In order to differentiate and to attract customers to use her services, a major telecommunication company in the United States designed and launched a new pricing scheme: flat phone pricing (i.e. one price regardless of how much time you spend on the phone). While the scheme was successful, the company found that they quickly ran out of resources in their exchange systems. This was because their subscribers were spending hours on the phone, jamming up their circuits. Some even spent days on the phone!

How can anyone spend days on the phone? The company investigated and found that many households were putting their phones to other use. Subscribers were using phones as baby monitors!

3M[29] developed its famous Post-it pads[30] in 1964 in its Polymers for Adhesives program in 3M's Central Research Laboratories. It developed an adhesive that was not very sticky but thought that there might be some moment when customers would want a glue to hold something for awhile but not forever. However, for many years, it found no use for this not-so-sticky glue until one of its researchers, a choir director, found its usage during a church choir practice! He would mark the songs he wanted to sing with slips of paper and discovered that the not-so-sticky adhesive, if put on a slip of paper, would become adhesive bookmarks.

Put to other use, the Post-it pads became one of the best selling products for 3M.

---

[29] http://www.3m.com/

[30] http://www.ideafinder.com/history/inventions/postit.htm

Questions to ponder:

▶ To solve your problem
- What products can be put to other use?
- What other products can be put to use to solve your current situation?

▶ To generate more revenue, what other uses can you put your products in to create a new market segment?

E- ELIMINATE

Eliminate is an excellent brainstorming keyword for cost savings and productivity related innovation projects. When you eliminate anything, you save cost, time, and resources. It is an extremely powerful way to drive efficiency.

What can you eliminate to save cost?

▶ Unpopular products or product options
▶ Unprofitable market segments from your portfolio
▶ Unprofitable customers (Ever thought of getting rid of them?)
▶ Tedious long-winded processes
▶ Obsolete rules and procedures, etc.

When I was working with HP, selling through resellers and channel partners were very important to us. Having lots of resellers means having lots of "feet on the streets" to push our products and services. Our entire business strategy revolved around resellers and channel partners. We would do lots of promotion in shopping malls, exhibitions, and PC shops.

None of us ever dreamt of a day when a 20-year-old kid could topple us by selling his PC through the web. Dell Computers[31] recognized that the market was paying for the overhead of the channel partners and provided direct sales and support to the end-users. Dell Computers was able to beat its competition by eliminating the expensive channels. Dell sold PCs by getting rid of the PC salesperson.

In short, Dell[32] sold PCs without PC shops! He eliminated the most important element in the old industry.

In the book industry, the most expensive (and yet the most critical) part of the value chain was the suppliers and the book stores. Book publishing and book selling are two sides of an inefficient business where the value chain of publishers, suppliers, and retailers are involved in conflicting intentions. Each party wants minimum risks (of demand prediction, printing, storing, displaying) and maximum returns in margin (minimum return of unsold books, discounts, and payment terms).

By selling books on the web, Amazon.com[33] eliminated the entire chain of middlemen to sell the books directly to the end consumers. While the largest brick-and-mortar bookstores and mail-order catalogs for books might offer 200,000 titles, an on-line bookstore like Amazon.com could offer a million more.

Through their Affiliate Network program, authors like me can sell my books to readers like you via Amazon.com (and other on-line bookstores) bypassing the entire chain in the reverse manner. Once again, businesses like Amazon.com[34] eliminated all the middlemen in between.

---

[31] Dell, Michael. w. (1999). Direct from DELL. Harper Collins Fredman.

[32] http://www.dell.com/

[33] Spector, R. (2000). Amazon.com, Get Big Fast. Harper Business.

[34] http://www.amazom.com/

The National Library Board (NLB)[35] of Singapore had a big problem. Prior to 1995, with 5.7 million visitors a year, it took an hour of queuing to return a book and another hour to borrow a book. With millions of frustrated readers, the library was nowhere near its vision of "inspiring lifelong learning".

What should they do to shorten the queue?

1. Increase the number of staff or
2. Chase away library users or
3. Build more libraries

The CEO, Dr. Christopher Chia, and his team brainstormed and invented a revolutionary "Book Drop" idea. To return books, customers simply throw their books into a "hole in the wall". Using Radio-Frequency Identification Technology (RFID)[36] , a scanner behind the wall detects the RFID tag on the returned book and releases it from the borrower. To borrow books, the customer uses a self-service counter. This system eliminated the need for staff to attend to users who want to borrow or return books, and thus resulting in considerable time savings. These counters are now an essential part of the NLB experience for library users.

An aggressive target of "zero wait time" for this innovation project was achieved. The project was a resounding success. In May 2002, when all the public libraries were fully equipped with RFID, the public's borrowing queue time was reduced to zero. This means the elimination of the queue totally. The achievement of "zero wait time" would translate to a saving of 11.4 million hours (assuming each visitor of the 5.7 million borrows a book) a year for their customers.

If NLB had aimed at a "zero wait time" without the RFID library system, more than 2000 additional staff would have been required. With the process

---

[35] http://www.nlb.gov.sg/

[36] Kuan, S. (2006). RFID What went right? What went wrong? Bibliotheksdienst 40. Jg. (2006), H. 8/9

fully automated, library staff can focus on providing valuable additional services such as assistance in matters of membership or enquiry, and helping readers to find their way to the books of their choice.

Questions to ponder:

▶ What is most important/critical element in your company or industry?
▶ Can you eliminate that?

If you can eliminate the most important element in your industry, you will stun your competitors. You will create the headlines in tomorrow's newspaper because you have created a brand new world.

R - REARRANGE

"Rearrange" is an excellent brainstorming key word for process related innovations. Using this keyword, you can deliberately rearrange your processes to see if things work more effectively.

LEARNING STEPS

Questions to ponder:

▶ How can I rearrange to achieve better results?
  ▪ Phrases in a project
  ▪ Priorities in business, customer services, account management, investment decisions, etc
  ▪ Sequence of workflow within a production line
  ▪ Blocks within an engineering diagram

- Procedures within a process
- Timing for execution of work instructions
- Logic within programming codes, etc

A good technique to use is to write each step (or block) of your process onto different pieces of memo pads or 3"x5" cards. Move them around and ask: "How can this new re-arrangement work better?" Continue playing and exploring different combinations and different sequencing. Take for example a restaurant dining process.

1. **Order, Eat, Pay**
   Customer enters a restaurant, orders what he wants, eat his meal, then pays for what he eats.

2. **Pay, Order, Eat**
   Customer pays a fixed price upon entering the restaurant, orders any item from the menu, then eats when the meal is served.

3. **Eat, Pay, Order for tomorrow**
   In an in-house employee canteen, or a restaurant he visits often, the customer eats (what he had ordered yesterday), pays for the meal, and orders for tomorrow (for cost efficiency so that the chef can buy the exact amount of ingredients, minimizing wastage)

4. **Eat, Order, Pay**
   The customer eats whatever he wants from the table (or from a moving conveyer belt in a Japanese restaurant). There is no ordering process. The billing process is simply counting the number of plates he has eaten, then the customer pays for what he eats.

5. **Order for the month, Pay, Eat, Eat, Eat**

    For families with dual working couples, nobody has the time to cook dinner for the family. Such customers can order from a menu by the month, pay for the entire month, and the family can eat and eat and eat throughout the month.

6. **Order, Eat, Pay, Pay, Pay**

    A customer takes his girlfriend to an expensive restaurant, has a wonderful meal, then pays and pays and pays to the credit card company.

Using just three boxes (Order, Eat, Pay), we can have six permutations of a business model. All of the above permutations are actual workable business models for the restaurant industry.

While we are having fun, let's try one more. When I was with Hewlett Packard, I experimented with the following processes to create new businesses. Take a look at the following typical sales cycle:

| Product Sales | Service Hotline | Repair Workshop | Logistics Spares | Post Warranty Service Sales |

1. Product Sales ⇨ Service Hotline ⇨ Repair Workshop ⇨ Logistics Spares ⇨ Post Warranty Service Sales (Original Process)

    ▶ First, a salesperson sells the product to a customer. During the warranty period, the customer calls the service hotline for repair whenever his product fails. The workshop repairs the product that uses spares from the logistics store. When the warranty period expires, the salesperson sells a post-warranty maintenance service to the customer.

2. Product Sales + Post Warranty Service Sales ⇨ Service Hotline Repair Workshop ⇨ Logistics Spares

   Selling both the product and extended post-warranty services together (creating a revenue stream for the company even before the product fails).
   ▶ Bundling the post-warranty service sales and selling the product with three years warranty instead of one year (borrowed this idea from the insurance industry).

3. Product Sales + Logistics Spares ⇨ Service Hotline ⇨ Repair Workshop ⇨ Post Warranty Service Sales

   ▶ Similarly, the salesperson can sell Products + Spares upfront for the customer to upgrade (more disk space or more memory in a PC or additional spares).

   ▶ Knowledgeable customers can do their own DIY repairs or upgrades.

4. Product Sales ⇨ Service Hotline ⇨ Repair Workshop ⇨ Logistics Spares ⇨ Product Sales

   ▶ After the warranty, the salesperson can sell a new, latest and greatest product instead of post-warranty service. E.g. when your mobile phone warranty runs out, it is time to buy a new phone.

   ▶ By putting sales at the end of the value chain, it prompts the thinking and triggering of
      i. Up-selling or upgrading of products or services
      ii. Cross-selling opportunities of other products or services
      iii. Product retirement, archiving, or disposition services
      iv. Data protection and transferring of data to new products

The permutations are endless. Actually a five-box process has 120 permutations, but it will seem endless if I try to write about all the possible permutations. You can brainstorm these permutations ideas and opportunities to explore what ways you can generate more revenue or save cost/time through process rearrangements.

R- REVERSE

Athletes around the world ran forward and jumped forward in an event called high jump. But one weirdo guy ran forward and jumped backward. The world laughed at him. Jumping backward went against all common logic and that young man was doomed to fail. In the 1968 Mexico City Olympics, Dick Fosbury[37] astonished the world with his "Fosbury Flop" to win the gold medal and set a new world record. Since then, all world class high-jumpers adopted his "reverse" jumping technique.

 "Reverse" means whatever you are (or the industry is) doing now, do it upside down or last step first. While it seems absurd to stand on your head at first, let's take a look at how we can use Reverse logic to help create new ideas.

Remember playing with your childhood puzzles and mazes? You were supposed to trace your path from a starting point to a destination. Halfway through the maze, you lost your way. You could start from the destination point and trace back to where you are. The same childhood reverse planning and tracing logic can be applied to our business thinking and planning.

When faced with a bottleneck in a process, what can you do? Can you reverse the process and start with other activities first? Do you have to go through a pre-defined process? Can we do things in the reverse order?

---

[37] http://en.wikipedia.org/wiki/Dick_Fosbury

LEARNING STEPS

Learning Steps

How do you do your annual business plan or project plan? We normally define where we are now (current position) and where we want to be next year in terms of our business objectives. In terms of action plans, we start our plan from Step 1 and work our way month by month towards the end of the work year or project.

Now, let's try reversing it.

Start from the end of the year, Month 12. What needs to be done by Month 12? Move your plan to Month 11. Then plan for Month 10 and continue your way backwards to Month 1. Do you see things in a different light?

In one of my planning workshop, I divided my participants into two groups. Group A planned forward and Group B planned backward. After an hour, the two groups met to discuss their plans. To their surprise, Group B was more thorough and saw more "loose ends" and pitfalls that Group A did not see. It is like driving and taking a peek at your rear view mirror to see where you have been.

Another way of reversing is to reverse the perspectives. We normally planned from **our own organization's perspectives** and from how we are going to launch and **sell our products** or service our customers. In the reverse perspectives, we can plan from our **customers' perspectives** and from how they are going to **use our products**. By planning from the customers' perspectives, we are able to understand them, to anticipate their needs, and to be able to service them better.

Taking the reverse logic further, can we reverse roles with our customers? Be your customer and walk in your customer's shoes for a day or a week. Don't just think about your customer, think like your customer. Behave like your customer. Buy your own products from the same shops as your customers. Use your own products and experience your own services like your customer. Pay like your customer from your own pocket. If you feel a pain paying from your wallet, your customers will feel the same pain too. Your product is possibly priced too high.

 When I was running the Product Service Center with HP, I encouraged all my country managers to try our own services as a customer. As one of our value-added services in Singapore, customers who need to repair their faulty notebooks can simply drop their notebooks into the nearest post office, instead of carrying them to the HP Service Center. Customers love the convenience as there is a post office within walking distance from every household. While the post office drop-off service sounded good theoretically, the taste of the pudding came when we tried to drop our own working notebook into the post office. Suddenly we hesitated because we were worried about the possible loss of data. What if the post office staff did not handle it properly? A thump might crash our hard disks, a bump may crack our LCD screen. What if the notebook goes missing? And if it rained, would the notebook get wet?

Once we reversed our roles and became the customer, we began to see and feel the pain of our customers. We began to be extra careful about the processes and the bubble-pack packaging and boxes to protect the notebooks. We trained the post office staff well. We checked and audited, checked and audited, until we ironed out all the kinks.

Try reversing roles between managers and staff (ouch!)

Try reversing roles between husband and wife (oops!)

CASE STUDY: REVERSE LOGIC FOR KILLING MOSQUITOES

About 30 years ago, I lived in a grand wooden house by the beach in Singapore. A grand house was a big house where several families live together under one roof. My grandparents, uncles, aunts, cousins, parents, and children all lived together. There must have been more than five families and about 30 people living under one roof. Each time a member of the family got married, all the males in the family would gather the planks, hammers, saws, and nails, and within a few days, they built an extension room for the newly-wed couple.

I lived with my parents in one such extension room. Hygiene was not good during those days. There were lots of puddles of stagnant water all around the neighborhood. Stagnant water breeds mosquitoes. Each night, hundreds of mosquitoes would invade our bedroom and I vividly recalled my mother clapping her palms throughout the night, killing mosquitoes. At the end of evening, my mum's palms would be colored black with mosquitoes' remains and red with the blood that they'd sucked. Despite her tireless effort, I still woke up each morning with over 30 bites on my limbs.

Mosquitoes are dangerous. They cause dengue[38] hemorrhagic fever. It is an acute viral infection transmitted to humans, and the symptoms include high fever, abdominal pain and vomiting, severe bleeding from the nose and gums, and even death. The Singapore government launched a massive campaign against mosquitoes, encouraging everyone to rid their homes of stagnant water, which is mosquito breeding ground.

30 years have flown by. I now have children of my own. Hygiene in Singapore is much better today. There were, however, still occasional

---

[38] http://en.wikipedia.org/wiki/Dengue

mosquito outbreaks in the neighborhood. Although there were much fewer mosquitoes than yesteryears, they were still the same horrible pesky mosquitoes biting my babies. Sub-consciously, I would chase after the mosquitoes, clapping away, doing what my mother used to do. Because there were much fewer mosquitoes, I seemed to have a much lower chance of finding and killing them. It was certainly a highly unproductive waste of time!

I had to think smarter, after all, mosquito brains aren't that big. Using reverse logic:

- ▶ Instead of killing them at NIGHT, would it be more effective to kill them in the DAY when visibility to us is better?
- ▶ Instead of chasing after the FLYING insect, could we kill it while it is STATIONARY?

A more effective way of killing mosquitoes was therefore to search for these mosquitoes in the day, when they were resting. Armed with a swapper, I began my proactive search for them in the day. Whenever I spotted one, I would creep up to it and gave it a good smack. The possibility of a kill was near 100%.

For years, the Government had been telling the citizens to empty pots, pails, and containers that might contain stagnant water to get rid of mosquito breeding grounds. Through their survival instinct, mosquitoes could still search, lay eggs, and survive in tiny puddles of water no larger than a dollar coin.

Testing the Reverse Logic further,

- ▶ Instead of GETTING RID of stagnant water, can we kill mosquitoes by KEEPING stagnant water?
- ▶ Instead of PREVENTING mosquitoes, can we kill mosquitoes by WELCOMING them into our house?

Certainly! Try this: Keep several containers filled with water under strategic spots where you are likely to find mosquitoes. Mosquitoes prefer dark corners, under bushes or behind furniture. Water takes several days to be stagnant. Take a look at these containers every two days for signs of eggs or wriggling larvae. Once found, empty the containers to kill the larvae. Then fill it up with fresh water and leave it for a few days. Repeat this filling and emptying of containers a few times and you can effectively get rid of the entire generation of mosquitoes.

Now instead of killing mosquitoes WHEN they suck our blood, we are even killing them BEFORE they can fly! But remember to always check on the water and empty the buckets before the larvae grow into mosquitoes!

Since we are in the mood of killing mosquitoes, let's try more reverse logic.

▶ Instead of SHOOING OFF the mosquitoes each time they buzz near you, can you kill them by ATTRACTING them to you?

I discovered this method accidentally. I have a treadmill at home and jog regularly while watching CNN. Once, as I sat to rest after a good workout, I saw a mosquito on my leg. Instinctively, I smacked it. A few seconds later, I found another and killed it as well. I soon realized that my sweaty smelly body was attracting these mosquitoes. I also realized that it was easier to smack the mosquitoes when they were attracted to you than if you were chasing after them. With reverse logic, I not only got rid of the mosquitoes in my house but for my entire neighborhood too.

Take Away Mosquito Learning:

▶ There are many ways to achieve the same objective and it need not be the same traditional way

Instead of	Try Reverse
Night	Day
Flying	Sleeping, Stationary
Getting Rid of	Keeping
Preventing	Welcoming
Shooing off	Attracting

Think of how you can apply Reverse thinking to solve problems in your workplace

▶ To save money
▶ To cut waste
▶ To improve operational efficiency
▶ To shorten the processing cycle

HUMANS INFECTING MOSQUITOES – THE REVERSE LOGIC

To kill mosquitoes in a big way, we need weapons of mass destruction, weapons that multiply within the mosquitoes themselves.

Researchers from Queensland University made a breakthrough that could curb the spread of dengue fever by shortening the life span of Aedes mosquito that spreads the disease[39] .

"The key is that only the very old mosquitoes are able to transmit the

---

[39] Straits Times, (2009, Jan 3). Dengue: Science bites back. Straits Times.

disease," said Professor Scott O' Neill[40] , head of biological sciences, Queensland University. "What we have done is to put this naturally occurring bacteria (Wolbachia bacterium) into the mosquitoes. That halves their adult lifespan so they do not live long enough to be able to transmit the virus."

Mosquitoes with the parasite lived only 21 days compared to 50 days for a regular mosquito. Once an insect is infected, the bacterium spreads via its eggs to the next generation. Well done, Professor! You have found a way to kill a parasite with another parasite!

► Instead of a mosquito infecting humans with dengue, we humans are infecting the mosquito with a virus.[41]

The reverse logic in innovation rules supreme!

BEYOND SCAMPER

We have provided you with numerous examples and case studies on how you can use the various keywords from SCAMPER to generate lots of ideas. Use them actively and frequently during your meetings, problem-solving sessions, and of course, innovation brainstorming sessions. Once you master the technique, you will find yourself far more creative than before. You will find ideas flowing like a running tap, unstoppable, without boundaries and without constraints. You will discover a brand new you.

What's next after SCAMPER?

---

[40] O'Neill, S., McMeniman, C., Lane, R., Cass, B., Fong, A., & Wang, M. S. (2009, Jan 2). Stable Introduction of a Life-Shortening Wolbachia Infection into mosquito Aede aegypti. Science Magazine , pp. 141-144.

[41] Andrew Read, M. T. (2009, Jan 2). Microbiology: Mosquitoes Cut Short. Science Magazine .

The key lessons we learnt from Innovation are:

- **Learn the Rules**

- **Master the Rules**

- **Throw away the Rules**

- **Invent your own Rules**

Key Point

Let's think of a letter not found in SCAMPER.

▶ Take the letter "B". Think of verbs beginning with "B". Verbs are action words that are easier to trigger "how to" ideas. From "B", we can generate words like: Borrow, or Balance, or Block.

- Who/where can we borrow the ideas from?
- How can we do this with borrowed resources?
- How can we balance the profits and the risk?
- How can we block the competitors from entering?
- How can we block the talent from leaving our organization?

▶ Taking the letter "D", we can think of Disperse, Destroy, Develop, Disintegrate, Displace, Dislocate, etc.

- In what ways can we disperse our products far and wide?
- How can we destroy our competitors' supply chain?
- What applications can we develop from this new device?
- How can we develop expertise for this new device?

The list goes on.

▶ Almost every verb in the dictionary can be used as a keyword to trigger ideas. Try it and have fun.

Besides verbs, can we use nouns? Of course we can. Let's try.

Say you want to find ways to cut cost. You think of "Apple". Thinking of apples, you can generate the following ideas:

▶ How to detect, isolate, and throw out rotten apples?
▶ Where are my juiciest apples that I must protect and retain?
▶ An apple a day keeps the doctor away. How to prevent apples from becoming rotten?
▶ Apple Pie, which part of my assets can I bake to convert them into something delicious for my customers?

You will find that using nouns to generate ideas is a little more difficult, but it is a lot more creative. Using nouns requires you to:

1. Find a co-relationship
   ▶ From apple to apple pie, rotten apples, Apple II, iPod, etc.

2. Using the co-relationship to generate ideas.

This double translation takes your mind further from the original innovation statements, and, as a result, you get wilder ideas. It's up to your imagination.

Although I mentioned that almost every word in the dictionary can be used as a trigger word for your brainstorming, do you really take any word randomly? Is there a more structured way of selecting trigger words?

BRAINSTORMING USING RELATED AND UNRELATED WORDS

From my experience, to have an effective brainstorming session, you need to select a combination of Related Words and Unrelated Words.

The **Related Words** help you generate lots of well-related ideas that are implementable, actionable, and practical. They help you focus on the task at hand and spawn out all possible ideas that the team should have thought of. These ideas include:

▶ "Quick win" ideas that you can do quickly to get early results.
▶ Haunting ideas – ideas that are at the back of your mind and everybody's minds
▶ Own Industry ideas, other industry ideas
▶ Ideas from competitors, ideas from other departments
▶ Routine ideas, obvious ideas, old ideas, etc

The **Unrelated Words** are true random words that you and your team can think of. Pick words that everyone in the team can relate to (apples, parachutes, Disneyland, yacht, riots, racing cars, etc). Do not use technical jargon that leaves your non-technical team out.   If technical jargon is essential, then they should be brainstormed under related words, with proper explanations for the non-technical folks to understand.

Ideas generated from unrelated words are usually:

▶ Weird, crazy, outrageously dumb
▶ Impractical, too expensive
▶ Blue sky ideas, dreams, fat hopes
▶ Ideas that will win you a slap and a kick from your boss

Use Unrelated Words as triggers or mind-joggers when you compose your ideas. Think of analogies and metaphors, stories and myths surrounding the verbs or nouns. Think of concepts and quotations. The ideas are limitless. Relate them to the innovation statement and create an idea from each of your thoughts.

If you can get any of these unrelated words ideas to work, you will have created a new world where there is no competitor. No competitor has ideas as weird as yours!

The stakeholder was the Regional Printer Ink Cartridge Sales Manager. He gathered a team together to generate ideas to grow ink cartridge sales. The team generated lots of ideas, amongst which were the following unrelated words:

1.   Christmas
2.   Fish

▶ What did Christmas have in relation to the printer ink cartridge sales?
▶ How could we increase ink cartridge sales during Christmas and other holiday seasons?

The idea was to excite the masses to print lots of Christmas greeting cards for their friends and use up a lot of ink, thereby generating more ink cartridge sales. In Japan, it became a trend to print personalized New Year cards as opposed to buying off-the-shelf New Year cards. HP detected this trend because there were more printer-related repair calls received than PC repair calls during each Christmas and New Year.

To leverage on this trend, HP packaged a free "Greeting Cards" software CD with every printer sold. Customers used the free software to print their personalized greeting cards, using up more ink and generating more ink cartridge sales.

▶ What did a fish have in relation to the printer ink cartridge sales?

HP developed a software program that used the number of pages you have printed as award points to generate fish food or accessories for the computer fish pet. The more pages you printed, the more points you scored. These scores will translate into different bonus. You will be able to use these points to exchange for seaweed or playthings for your computer pet fish. This idea created a lot of excitement among the customers. While it was necessary to print out the documents, the customers had more fun with printing. Of course, the company was very excited with the increased printer ink cartridge sales too!

Learning Steps

LEARNING STEPS

How to brainstorm with related and unrelated words?

The Facilitator :

1. Writes the Innovation Statement on the whiteboard (or flipchart or Powerpoint). He or the Innovation Owner explains the objectives, the situation background, and makes sure everyone understands the Innovation Statement.

2. Invites the team to shout out 20 Related Words and writes each one on the whiteboard.

3. Explains the Silent Brainstorming process and starts the clock ticking for seven to 10 minutes.

4. When the team slows down and runs out of ideas, the facilitator can switch gear to Unrelated Words. Once again, he invites the team to shout out 20 unrelated words, which he writes on the whiteboard.

5. Once again, he starts the silent brainstorming process and the clock. Allow extra time for the unrelated words as they are more difficult to use in generating ideas.

Note: Always brainstorm Related Words first as they are easier. You can use it to warm up the team and for them to dump all the ideas in their brain onto the memo pads before the real creative ones can emerge through Unrelated Words.

"WHAT-IF?" TECHNIQUE

"What If?" is a great technique to use for generating blue skies ideas. This technique knows no bounds. It tickles your fantasies and takes you to a world where dreams may come true. It brings you out from the world of reality to the world of possibilities and opportunities.

"What-if" statements:

- ▶ What if power cords are wireless?
- ▶ What if my notebooks can be recharged anytime anywhere?
- ▶ What if we can build zero-energy homes?
- ▶ What if bicycle wheels are square?

Once we can imagine the possibilities of the future, we will be excited to create the new world. The "What If" Technique can be used to generate Innovation Statements, followed by the generation of lots of ideas on the "How to" to make the "What if" statements come true.

"What-if" Innovation Statements:

- ▶ What if my refrigerator can tell me that we are running out of milk?

Possible Ideas:

- ■ We can put bar-code scanners inside the fridge so that the fridge "knows" what is in and what's not.

- ■ We can have a weight sensor to tell us if the milk carton is below 25% weight.

- We can put a computer chip in the fridge so that we can instruct the fridge what to keep track of, when to alert us that the stock is running low, to check on expiry dates, etc.

- We can link the fridge to the internet to order groceries on-line from the neighborhood supermarket.

- We can put odor sensors in the fridge to detect and alert us if any food item is going bad.

Interesting? Let's try one more.

"What-If" Innovation Statement:

▶ What if my toilet bowl can think and talk?

Possible Ideas:

- Linked to a computer, the toilet bowl can greet me and remind me my schedule for the day every morning when I sit on my throne.

- It can analyze the "stuff" that comes out from me and tell me if I am in good health, if I am lacking some nutrients, or if I need to rush down to my doctor for a full-blown cancer check-up.

- Depending on whether my "stuff" floats or sinks, it can remind me to eat more vegetables.

- It can also track and plot trends of my sugar level, calories, and cholesterol.

- By the way, since I am sitting on it, it should be able to tell me my weight.

FIREWORKS – A SPARK OF INNOVATION

The 2008 Beijing Olympics[42] opened with a burst of color and splendor as fireworks lit the night skies and the TV screens around the world. I was awed with wonder as splashes of color, changing hues and shapes danced before my eyes. I noticed two innovations here. For the first time, the world saw fireworks in the shape of the Olympic rings symbol and welcoming smiley faces. This prompted me to do some research on Chinese fireworks innovations.

Fireworks and gunpowder were invented by the Chinese dating back to the 6th Century[43] . There were two legends about how fireworks were discovered or invented by the Chinese. One legend described how a Chinese cook working in a field kitchen accidentally happened to mix charcoal, sulphur, and saltpeter (all commonly found in the kitchen in those days). He ignited the compound and caused an explosion in the kitchen. He further experimented with the compounds and tried different ways of packaging it. He placed them in a shell, wrapped it up, added a fuse, and voilà, firework was invented.

The second story is about a group of Taoists who were trying to make that "immortal elixir" for the emperor. They were experimenting with different substances and mixing them into the elixir urn to be super-heated over many hours. As part of their experiment, they happened to mix agricultural fertilizers (due to its plant nourishment qualities) with sulphur (due to the belief that it has the ability to remove poison/toxins). The potassium (K) and phosphorous (P) in the fertilizer reacted with sulphur in the heat, which caused a huge explosion.

---

[42] http://en.beijing2008.cn/

[43] Jack, K. Gunpowder: Alchemy, Bombards, and Pyrotechnics: the History of Explosive that Changed the World. New York: Basic Books, Perseus Books Group.

During festive celebrations, the Chinese used smaller, controlled doses of these explosives as firecrackers to ward off evil spirits. That was how firecrackers and fireworks came about.

Let's see how SCAMPER can be (or had been) applied in the development and continuous innovation of fireworks:

▶ Put to Other Use:

 ■ For a different purpose: Warfare instead of festive celebration
  ⇨ The great destructive power of fireworks was put to use in destroying enemy forces during war.

  ⇨ Early records showed the Chinese using the firework gunpowder in warfare. In 1232, Chinese troops used fireworks, packed into bombs that were catapulted onto the Mongol troops besieging Kaifeng, capital of the north Chinese Jin Empire. During the later years of the 13th century, the Chinese invented cannons, using gunpowder to fire projectiles from metal barrels.

 ■ In a different country
  ⇨ One of the first recorded applications of gunpowder in European military history occurred at the 1346 Battle of Crecy, where the English arsenal included little gunpowder "firepots."

▶ Substitute /combine
 ■ By substituting and combining different chemicals, such as sodium, aluminum, magnesium, and titanium, fireworks can display different beautiful brilliant colors.

▶ Modify
 ■ Make it smaller and wrap it around a stick, and you get sparklers.

- Tie a tube of fireworks to a stick or an arrow, and you get rockets.
- Make it portable, and it can be use as signal flares or road flares.

► Eliminate

- Where there's fire, there's smoke. Smoke is annoying and is a health hazard. The Chinese inventors added Nitrocotton and Perchlroric Acid to create smokeless fireworks, which is more environmental friendly and can be used indoors, like disco dance floors and on the wedding stage[44].

- Fireworks have debris. Eliminate debris and smoke, and now you can have fireworks safe enough to light up your birthday cake[45].

► Adapt /Modify

- To a different environment – Water
  Who said fireworks must be on dry land? A common reaction would be that water would extinguish fire. The Chinese thought about this problem and modified it to make fireworks waterproof.

- Continuing to innovate further, they put the fireworks into a tube that could float on water. Now fireworks could be ignited from lakes, rivers, and seas. The combination of fire and water on flowing rivers and sparkling lakes makes the entire fireworks display both awesome and mystic. Reflection over water doubles the impact of such spectacular displays.

- Modify its form and shape to form letters
  "Subtitle fireworks" is a modification and an adaptation

---

[44] Walt Disney Company. (2004, june 28). Disney debuts new safer, quieter, and more environmentally-friendly fireworks technology . Press release.

[45] Stoddard, D. (2006, July 14). Fireworks: safer than candles, tableware. Sacramento Ledger Dispatch

of fireworks by skillfully arranging them to spell out your company's name and form the logo to grace corporate events.

► Adapt/modify/combine
- ■ Adapt to a different environment – Daytime
  - ⇨ Why must we wait for nightfall before watching fireworks? How can we make daytime events more stunning?

  - ⇨ The answer is daytime fireworks! Add oxidizers and you turn the fireworks into brilliant colored smoke.

- ■ Combined with toys and confetti
  - ⇨ Add these toys to fireworks and you fill up the sky with hundreds of floating flags, parachutes, lanterns, and little flying saucers.

- ■ Combine with computers, music, and lots of imagination
  - ⇨ You get the dazzling, jaw-dropping synchronized display worthy of the historic 2008 Olympics Opening Ceremony

Having read how innovation can contribute to shaping the history of fireworks, how can innovation help you shape the future of your products and services?

We have shared several brainstorming techniques with you. You can select whichever method you find most effective or comfortable to use. Before trying this out with your group, try out the methods yourself. Practice and you will be fluent.

SUMMARY

Summary Notes

1. When generating ideas, strive for both volume and uniqueness.

2. When brainstorming, always think concurrently, not serially.

3. Brainstorming Techniques
    a. SCAMPER as trigger words:
        i.   Substitute words, roles, materials
        ii. Simplify processes, rules, shortcuts, number of steps, decisions
        iii. Combine features, roles, parts, products
        iv. Adapt to another industry, purpose, geography, market
        v.   Modify products, services, options
        vi. Put to other use or purpose
        vii. Eliminate unpopular products, markets, customers, processes
        viii.Rearrange your workflow, processes, project phases, priorities
        ix. Reverse your planning processes, roles, perspectives, actions

    b. Use a combination of Related and Unrelated Words to generate more ideas

    c. Use "What-if" technique to explore possible creative scenarios of the future

4. Golden rules in innovation:

    a. Learn the rules
    b. Master the rules
    c. Throw away the rules
    d. Invent your own rules

CHAPTER 7
IDEAS SELECTION

"It's an Ideas Selection Tool."

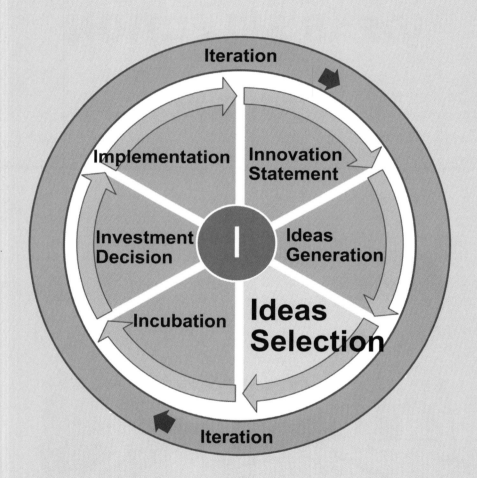

CHAPTER 7: IDEAS SELECTION

We had so much fun the day before spawning ideas after ideas. We remembered that ideas must flow like clear running water, so it flows and floods. We wake up the next day with a thousand pieces of ideas on memo pads on our table. A thousand! What are we going to do with these ideas? How are we going to sort them out?

In the Ideas Generation Phase, we invite and welcome anyone and everyone to join in and contribute ideas. This is because we want as many ideas as possible. However, in the Ideas Selection Phase, **only the people who are ACCOUNTABLE and RESPONSIBLE (Innovation Owner and the Innovation Team) are involved in selecting the ideas.** This is for the purpose of **COMMITTMENT.** The team is accountable for the success of the project and responsible for the implementation of the ideas. Therefore the owner and the team have to make the ultimate decision on which ideas to implement.

Let's say we want to go for a field trip to study animals. Which options do you choose?

1. The zoo
2. The local natural reserve
3. The Amazon jungle

If you just want to have a fun day with your children, a trip to the zoo would suffice. If you want to take a few days of holiday break from routine work to study nature or to be with nature, then going to the local nature reserve makes sense. You may encounter occasional danger from wild animals (like snakes and scorpions), but generally, nature reserves are quite safe.

However, if you want headline news when you discover new species or capture rare animals on video or the interest of National Geographic to film you wrestling with the carnivorous Amazon warriors, then an adventure in the Amazon will fulfill your dreams. Note that the snakes that you find may be rib-crushing anacondas!

The choice selection depends on who you are, your current knowledge level about animals, and the purpose of your field trip. It also depends on your aptitude and appetite for risk, intrigue and adventure. The team accountable to embark on the journey (which Innovation Project to embark on) will be the one that makes the final decision (which ideas to implement). This ensures commitment.

I would like to introduce a few sorting techniques in this chapter:
► Voting
  ■ Suitable for sorting out 10-50 ideas

► Perspectives and Criteria Matrix (PCM[46])
  ■ Suitable for sorting out 50 to 1000 ideas

LEARNING STEPS

Learning Steps   **VOTING**

Your team has 10 to 50 ideas (each written on a little memo pad) to choose from. Because the quantity is relatively small, the team can afford time to brainstorm and discuss each of the ideas in greater detail. The Facilitator can mediate the meeting to make sure that everyone has a chance to voice their views.

The Facilitator tells the team that each member has five votes, which they can cast by giving a tick (or writing their initials) on the ideas they like. The memo pads are spread across the table so that everybody can see and read them. Discussions are permitted. A member can cast a vote each for five separate ideas that he likes or he can cast more votes on his favorite idea (even all five votes on the same idea).

At the end of the voting session, the facilitator consolidates the votes and highlights the top few ideas with the most votes. This process can repeat until the team is happy with the ideas selected by the group.

The figure of five votes is arbitrary. It depends on the number of people present and the number of ideas to be selected. The concept is that there must be enough votes on the ideas to form vote clusters, where the favorite ideas clearly stand out from the rest.

PERSPECTIVE-CRITERIA MATRIX SORT (PCM)

Beyond 50 ideas, it will be impractical to discuss and cast votes. We need to:

▶ Synchronize everybody's thinking
▶ Use a more efficient and CONCURRENT technique

To synchronize everybody's thinking, we need to discuss and decide on:

▶ What perspectives
▶ What selection criteria

PERSPECTIVES

The word "Perspective" comes from a Latin word, "perspicere", which means to see through. It is the angle from which we look at things or the position we adopt mentally when we view a certain situation, issue, or idea.

Perspective in the graphic arts, such as drawings, is a representation, on a flat surface (such as paper), of an image as it is perceived by the eye of the artist. It shows us the appearance of things relative to one another as determined by their distance and position from the viewer. An ice-cream cone appears like a circle from the top view and an upside-down triangle from the side view.

In the proverbial story of five blind men who touched different parts of an elephant, the first man touched the elephant's trunk and said that an elephant looked like a snake, while the second touched the elephant's leg and said that the elephant looked like a tree trunk. The remaining three touched the body, the ear, and the tail and remarked that the elephant looked like a wall, a fan, and a whip respectively.

To avoid the mistakes of the five blind men in the story, we need to examine our ideas from different perspectives before we can make decisions regarding the selection of our ideas.

LEARNING STEPS

Whose perspectives should we be looking from?

The stakeholders – people who are affected by the innovation

Examples:

► The company, employer, management, shareholders
► The staff, workers
► The other departments, colleagues (sales, marketing, product development, manufacturing, operations, support, administration, legal, etc)
► The customers (past, current, and future)
► The market, competitors (past, current, and future)
► The government, authority, regulators
► The partners, channels
► The environment, etc

Let's say that we have a problem:

"The economy is bad and the sales orders are down."

► One idea is to retrench 10% of the workers to cut cost. It's an excellent idea from the employer's perspective but a terrible idea for the affected employees.

► Another idea is to cut everybody's salary by 10% to stay afloat. A better idea for the employees (although still painful), the same amount of savings for the employer.

> ▶ The third idea is to innovate by finding different ways to use the product, selling products to different markets, working with different channel partners to push the products to different countries. This idea will stimulate growth, and now gets rid of the problems in the earlier ideas. This is a win-win idea for both the employer and the employees.

As illustrated, by considering different perspectives, we can select the best ideas that satisfy the needs of multiple stakeholders. To ensure success and acceptance for your innovation project, it is important to select sets of **balanced perspectives**. Examples:

▶ Internal versus external
▶ Management versus staff
▶ Customers or partners versus company
▶ Sales versus post-sales support

SELECTION CRITERIA

To select the best ideas from a big pile of hundreds, we need to define what our selection criteria are. Selection criteria are defined as:

▶ Attributes, guidelines, rules, characteristics, or dimensions that are used to judge the quality and relevance of our ideas
▶ Standards that we use as a basis for comparison
▶ A reference point against which other ideas can be evaluated

Examples of selection criteria are:
▶ Degree of innovativeness
▶ Most important
▶ Most urgent
▶ Fastest speed of implementation

► Ease of usage
► Lowest cost
► Shortest time to market
► Highest value added to customers
► Degree of acceptance by customers
► Degree of implementation risks
► Least amount of resources, etc

DECIDING ON THE PERSPECTIVE – CRITERIA MATRIX

Take an example. We are looking for ideas for new product development to bring in more revenue and we brainstormed 100 ideas using the Ideas Generation Techniques discussed in the previous chapters. To select the best ideas, we need to decide on:

► Two perspectives
► Two selection criteria per perspective

Step 1:

For our case of selecting new product development ideas, go through the list of perspectives, and discuss with your team to see which two makes most sense. Let's assume you and your team select:

► Customers' perspective
► Company's perspective

Step 2:

For each of the perspectives, select two criteria
Looking through the criteria list, we can select:

► Customer's perspective:
  ■ Highest Important and

■ Most Urgent needs

▶ Company's perspective:
  ■ Easiest to implement with
  ■ Minimum risk

Step 3:

(1) Draw the two (2p x 2c) Perspectives and Criteria matrixes on a large flip chart paper.

(2) For Customers' Perspective, place one criterion (say Most Important) on the horizontal axis and the other (say Most Urgent) on the vertical axis.

Urgency ↑		
Rank 3 Most Urgent Least Important	Rank 4 (BEST) Most Important Most Urgent
Rank 1 (Worst) Least important Least urgent	Rank 2 Most important Least Urgent

Importance →

(3) Rank the boxes where 4 is the best and 1 is the worst idea.

(4) Together with your team members, sort out the 100 ideas into the four quadrants.

(5) Remember that we had intentionally left the top 2 cm of our memo pad blank (see page 107)? After your sort, write the rank (1 to 4) on the ideas memo pad, depending on which quadrant they belong to.

(6) Repeat the same process for the other perspective (i.e. Company). In this case, the Company's perspective matrix looks like this:

Risk	Rank 2 Easiest to implement Most Risk	Rank 1 (Worst) Difficult to Implement Most Risk
	Rank 4 (BEST) Easiest to Implement Least Risk	Rank 3 Difficult to Implement Least Risk

Implementation Difficulty

(7) Document this second set of ranking on the ideas memo pad.

(8) Add the two sets of numbers. Those ideas scoring 4 + 4 = 8 represent the best ideas (i.e. Most Urgent, Most Important from the Customer's Perspective, and Easiest to Implement and Least Risk from the Company's perspective). The next best set of ideas scored 7 marks, and so forth.

(9) Mathematically, sorting 100 ideas using 2 x 2 x 2 matrices will give you about 12 to 13 best ideas. This number is small enough for us to do detailed discussion and planning in the incubation phase.

Notice that while it is easy to understand which quadrant is the best (Rank 4) and which is the worst (Rank 1), it is not obvious to decide on the Rank 2 and 3 position. Let the team debate on which is more critical from the customer's perspective (Urgent or Important), and which from

Company's perspective (Risk or Implementation Ease), then allocate the rank accordingly.

I chose to place Urgency higher than Importance as customers are more willing to pay a higher price for something they need immediately compared to something important but for which they can afford to wait. Risk is a factor of corporate management culture and attitude while Ease of Implementation is a factor of employee expertise and resources. Select one over the other.

As we employ concurrent thinking methods, do expect a fair number of duplicate ideas. This is the stage where duplicate ideas are discarded. Some of the "quite similar" ideas may be phrased differently or adapted or modified from each other. These "quite similar" ideas, which may be useful at a later stage, can be stapled together so that they can be sorted as ONE idea.

VARIATION OF PCM

The two perspectives and two criteria described above form the basics of idea selection. Once you understand and master the PCM technique, you can vary it to suit the needs of different projects, different requirements, and different innovation statements. Some of my frequently used variations are as follows:

Ranking:

▶ If the team feels that the ranks of 1, 2, 3, 4 do not accurately reflect the relative criticalness in the selection criteria, you can change it to 1, 2, 3, 6 or 1, 2, 4, 8, etc, where more critical boxes in the matrix get more points.

▶ If the two criteria are really equal, you can modify the rank to 4, 2, 2, 1.

Weight:

▶ If one criterion is more critical than the other, you can place different weights on the different criteria. Multiply the corresponding rank by an appropriate weight value.

Scale:

▶ Instead of just 2 x 2 matrixes, where one extreme is most and the other extreme is least, you can change the scale to "High, Medium, Low". You end up with a 3 x 3 matrixes where the best ideas get the highest of 9 points.

▶ Similarly extending the scale from 1 to 5 will give you 25 boxes.

Perspectives:

▶ What happens when you have more than two perspectives? Let's say you want to sort from customer AND company AND employee perspectives. Simply create one more matrix and sort one more round (3p x 2c).

Criteria:

▶ What if you have more than two criteria per perspective? Just add one more matrix (2p x 3c). Exercise: Try drawing it – you need some imagination to do this.

As you can see, the PCM is very flexible. Using the concept of PCM, you can sort out 100 or 1000 ideas into a manageable, implementable few. The ideas are ranked by your perspectives and selection criteria.

Do not throw away your low ranking ideas during your selection process. By varying the perspectives and the criteria, and doing a re-sort, you will end up with different sets of selected ideas.

Try it and have fun.

PCM ALIGNMENT

In his book on 7 Habits[47] , Stephen Covey stated, "begin with the end in mind". I have intentionally positioned this paragraph at the end of the chapter to illustrate the need to begin with the end in mind. Unless you have a fat wallet, you need to search for someone with a fat wallet to fund your innovation project.

Caution!

Important questions to ask BEFORE selecting your Perspectives and Criteria are:

- **WHO is going to fund your project?**

- **HOW are you going to get management approval or investment funding?**

- **Which perspectives are the approving management team and/or funding authorities looking from?**

- **What criteria are they considering to evaluate your innovation project?**

- **Under what conditions will they approve the investment funding?**

- **What is the level of Return-On-Investment required?**

---

[47] Covey, Stephen. (2003). The 7 Habits of Highly Effective People. Simon & Schuster.

To better position yourself for the "YES" approval, your Perspective-Criteria Matrix must be aligned with your management's/investors'/sponsors' requirements.

SUMMARY

Summary Notes

1. While everyone can be involved in the Ideas Generation phase, only the people who are ACCOUNTABLE and RESPONSIBLE for the project will be involved in the Ideas Selection phase (the Innovation Owner and the Implementation Team).

2. Two ideas selection techniques
   a. Voting
      i. Each member is given a number of votes that he casts to select his favorite ideas. The ideas with the most votes win.

   b. Perspectives – Criteria Matrix
      i. Brainstorm the different perspectives and criteria needed to select the ideas
      ii. Select two perspectives and two criteria per perspective
      iii. Draw a Perspective-Criteria Matrix based on one perspective
      iv. Sort out and rank the ideas
      v. Repeat with the other perspective

   c. Vary the number of perspectives or criteria as needed

   d. Make sure you align your PCM with the stakeholders' requirements
      i. Begin with the end in mind

CHAPTER 8
INCUBATION

"Wrong mountain. Incubation is on the other side."

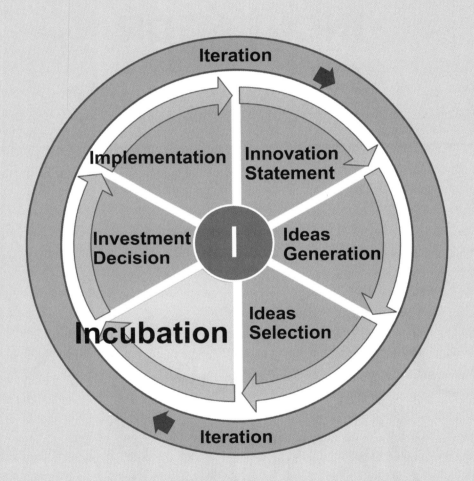

CHAPTER 8: INCUBATION

A baby was born. Not any baby, but your special baby. Your one and only pride and joy. From the moment he smiled at you, you knew that this child had tremendous potential. He had a bright future ahead. He could change the way we work, the way we play, and he had the opportunity to change the world. You were very excited. With everything that you had, you wanted to nurture this child to his full potential.

But wait, this is a very young infant. Very weak and vulnerable. He is not ready, perhaps premature, to face the world. What are you going to do? You put him into an incubator, carefully and patiently nursed him and fed him. Gradually (and hopefully), the baby grew stronger and more capable of running on his own.

This baby was, of course, your breakthrough idea. You had sorted out 1000 ideas to a handful of 12-13 best workable ideas. These formed your baby. It is now time to develop these ideas further in the Incubation Phase.

What is incubation?

There are three meanings to this word.

> ► From the innovation point of view, this is the process phase where the team ponders through the ideas at hand, enhancing them and developing them to make them stronger.

> ► From the business perspective, this is a time to hand-hold new startup companies.

> ► From the medical perspective, it is the time when newborn babies are looked after round the clock to ensure that they are stable and healthy before they are turned over to the mother's care. (It is also

the time between being exposed to infection and showing the first symptoms).

What do we do during the Incubation Phase?

The two main tasks are:

1. Ideas Development and Enhancement
2. Data gathering/fact finding

IDEAS DEVELOPMENT AND ENHANCEMENT

During the Ideas Generation phase, each idea written on a memo sheet contains merely a few words or a phrase. They survived the Ideas Selection phase as they were ranked high in terms of the selected criteria from the various perspectives.

This is the time to develop and enhance each of these selected ideas further using the P.E.N.S[48] technique.

LEARNING STEPS

For each of the selected ideas, the team brainstorms the following questions:

P - Positive, Plus, Potentials

▶ What are the **positive** aspects of this idea?
▶ What are the **plus** points and advantages?

---

[48] P.E.N.S. Copyright © 2009 John Seah

▶ What are the **potentials** that this idea can bring?

Think along the line of
- "I like this idea because …"
- "I am really excited that this idea has the potential to …"

E - Enhancement, Excitement, What Else?

▶ How can we enhance the idea further?
▶ How can we make this idea more exciting?
▶ What else can we add to make this idea even stronger?
▶ How else can we use it?
▶ Where else can we apply/sell it?

This section itself can be an exciting brainstorming session to enhance the selected ideas further. Consider spin-offs, out-of-the-box potentials, new market segments, etc. Let ideas flow. Leave no stone unturned.

N - Negative, Not

▶ What are the negative aspects of this idea?
▶ Which aspect of this idea does not add value and can be removed?
▶ Which aspects do the customers/stakeholders not want?

Use this section to capture all the negative aspects of the ideas. The intention is to hear and consider all the pitfalls and dangers so that we can find solutions to avoid. Capture whatever the team is uncomfortable about. In a way, we are trying to identify potential risks and weaknesses so as to develop actions to counter the dangers proactively.

► What may possibly go wrong?
► Where are our areas of vulnerability?
► What are some of the difficulties that could occur?

S - Solutions

Taking into consideration the P.E.N. above,
► What solutions can we come up with to turn this idea into a breakthrough?
► How can I remove all the constraints, obstacles, and roadblocks highlighted under "N"?
► Consider potential solutions for possible pitfalls and obstacles.
► Get your team to focus on solutions and answers. No more problems, no more buts.

This is the part where ideas can be re-shaped and re-moulded into something stronger and more enticing.

Many possible solutions may be generated at this stage. Do keep your ideas aligned to your Innovation Statement objectives and select the best match.

PENS is an excellent Incubation technique for bullet-proofing your ideas. It evaluates your ideas holistically from both the positive and negative aspects and then brainstorms solutions to proceed.

Brainstorm around scenarios such as: "What might happen if...?" to identify the areas in your plan of action that could potentially:

► Enhance the value or potential of your idea
► Avoid areas that may cause your idea to fail

A DAY IN THE LIFE OF THE CUSTOMER

An innovation is useless if there is no customer. Not only do we want customers to buy our innovation, we want them to use it, to love it, and to tell the world how great our innovation is.

Once again, we need to begin with the end in mind. Who are your customers? It seems like an obvious question. Let's probe further:

▶ Are the customers for your Innovation Project internal or external to your organization?
▶ Are your customers the management or the end-users?
▶ Are your users generic (for Administration or Clerical) or specialized (like a dietician or telemetry systems designer)?
▶ Who is the decision maker for your innovation? Are they the procurement manager or the end consumers or senior management?

Brainstorm with your team. Do not stop at the first obvious customer. Probe further and you may end up with a list of 10-20 possible customers or potential customer segments. Prioritize them and select three to five customers who have the most impact in making a buying or using decision for your innovation.

Consider customer's customers. Examples:

▶ A father (customer) buying a toy for the child (customer's customer) to play: The innovative toy must be educational, safe, and affordable (father's selection criteria), and at the same time, attractive and fun (child's selection criteria).

▶ A computer systems should be affordable (within the purchasing manager's budget), easy to use (user's department's selection criteria), and produce high value for the company (CEO's selection criteria).

Consider the various customers throughout the entire supply chain or value chain:

- ▶ **Developer:** The product must be easy to design, develop, and manufacture.
- ▶ **Logistics:** it must easy to pack, store, and transport.
- ▶ **After-sales support:** easy to repair, good diagnostics.
- ▶ **Management:** product must add value to my business. Either it helps me grow my business or helps me save money.
- ▶ **End User:** Easy to use, reliable, and durable.

The technique is to imagine you as one of the customers.

1. Imagine walking in your customer's shoes for a day. Mentally walk through the steps that you need to go through when you execute a task (or do your daily work) using the innovative product. Any sub-tasks to perform before, during, and after using your product?

2. Imagine a new user seeing and working with your innovation for the first time. Is it user friendly? Are the functions intuitive?

3. Think of all your Positive "P" and Enhancement "E" points. Are they being enjoyed by your customers? How do your "P" and "E" points enhance your customers' experience or make their work better?

4. Think of all your Negative "N" points. Are they being removed? Anticipate the problems that a customer/user will face when using your innovation.

5. Think of all your Solution "S" points. Do they truly solve your customer's problems?

6. If you can, make a quick prototype of your innovation, give it to a couple of actual users, and watch how they use it. Interview them and document their comments and feedback.

A company specializing in fertilizers wanted to launch a new brand of fertilizer. They gave a few samples to a selected group of farmers to try. They experimented with various packaging and different compositions of chemicals. The new product did not sell very well.

To investigate why, the company dispatched a group of executives to act as farmers. They performed all the farming chores for a couple of weeks. The executives realized the complexity of different soil conditions for different crops needed different combinations of chemicals to produce the best yield. So they called their colleagues to bring down their state-of-the-art instruments to perform soil analysis to determine the best chemical composition.

At the end of their "Day in the Life of your Customer" experience, the executives realized that the complexity was a nightmare, the packaging of fertilizers did not matter, and even the fertilizers did not matter. In the minds of the farmers, what mattered most was better crop yield from the land.

As a breakthrough thinking innovation, the company launched a new "we-do-it-for-you" service that analyzed the soil and applied the right combination of chemicals on behalf of the farmers. That new service became an instant hit amongst the farming community.

KNOWING YOUR DATA

Incubation is the time to gather data that supports (or challenges) your ideas. Your stakeholders and customers are vital sources of data. Plan to survey them, visit them, and interview them. Points to take note of when gathering data:

▶ Understand if the data is actual or observed.
▶ Are they objective or subjective?

- ▶ Are they the customer's interpretation of events or are they facts?
- ▶ Does the data change over time?
- ▶ What's related and what's not?
- ▶ Make sure you cover the 5W 1H (what, who, where, when, why, and how)
- ▶ Gather raw data from the customer's perspectives. Understand them from his language (industry domain specific) and knowledge level (basic generic or technical).
- ▶ Is the data reproducible and measurable?

With the data collected, does the data support your ideas?

OR does the data prove otherwise?

INCUBATION PERIOD

Have you ever fallen in love? Are you still in love the morning after? What about a month or a year later? Time removes blind emotions and spur-of-the-moment decisions. Many times, people put down deposits for a lovely condominium or an expensive car only to regret it the very next day. Love at first sight happens to innovators too.

The medical folks define the Incubation Period as the time elapsed between the exposure to a virus or an infection or chemical or radiation and when symptoms are first apparent.

In innovation, the incubation period is a timeframe that allows our emotions to cool down and our mind to be rational. Rational minds think differently from the emotional passion of the heart. The rational mind focuses on the practical aspect of the innovation[49].

Leave the grand idea alone for a period of time. Does the passion

---

[49] Christensen, T. B. (2005). Creative Cognition: Analogy and Incubation. University of Aarhus, Denmark.

disappear? Does it seem dumb the next morning? Or is it still a shiny star worthy of your investment of time and resources?

Ideas get consolidated and polished over time. A few days' of incubation time gap allows both the conscious and the subconscious brain to cross-check and to ponder over the nights. The outcome usually will be stronger.

During the medical latency period, a disease carrier may be contagious. During the innovation latency period, the innovator can infect his colleague and get them to be excited about the innovation project. Or his colleague can cure him out of his madness.

SUMMARY

Summary Notes

1. Incubation is about nurturing, enhancing, and strengthening your ideas before commitment of resources.

2. Use PENS technique:
   a. Positive, Plus, Potentials
   b. Enhancement, Excitement, Else
   c. Negative, Not
   d. Solutions

3. Experience "A day in the life of your customer" using your innovation. Watch, learn, and improve.

4. Understand your data.

5. Set aside an incubation period to consolidate your ideas and polish them over time.

CHAPTER 9
INVESTMENT
DECISION

"If you are planning for a year, sow rice;
if you are planning for a decade, plant trees;
if you are planning for a lifetime, invest in innovation."

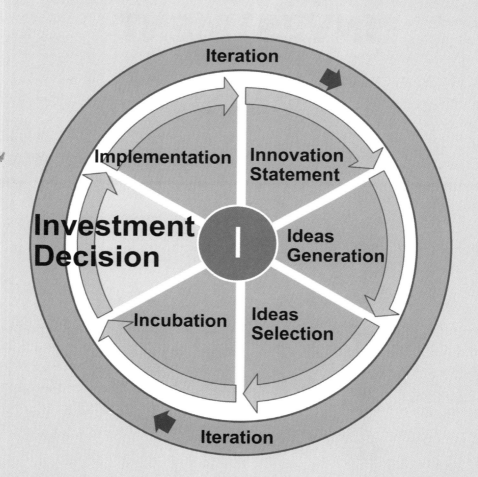

CHAPTER 9: INVESTMENT DECISION

We watched week after week, contestants after contestants, presenting their inventions to the panel of judges in the American Inventor[50] competition. American Inventor was a reality television series based on a search for America's best inventor, aired by American Broadcasting Company[51] (ABC). Many participants believed that their products would sell millions, and invested years of effort and their entire life savings into their so-called inventions, which they passionately thought would conquer the world by storm.

In one episode, a contestant named Vivek who presented a "Sit and Shave" that could not even survive one minute before all the three judges booted him out. His invention was a container for the shaving cream with a mirror. His value proposition was saving time. While his invention was useful, it was certainly not innovative at all.

Some of the inventions that failed to impress the judges ranged from a Pet Patter (to pat your dog when you are at work) to a Bladder Buddy (a wrap-around cover so that you can pee in the public if you cannot find a toilet) to a SkaterTrainer (a device that looked like a baby walker, which ensures a novice skater does not fall). All these gadgets received thumbs down from the judges, much to the disappointment of the inventors who had just thrown away their investments and years of hard work. No doubt each of these inventions was useful, but they failed to meet the grade miserably.

What went wrong?

Does the problem lie with their inventions or their presentations?

---

[50] http://en.wikipedia.org/wiki/Americian Inventor.

[51] http://www.abc.com/

How can the contestants avoid such expensive mistakes if they were given another chance?

What can you learn from them to avoid making their mistakes?

What differentiates the winners from the losers?

WHAT TO LOOK OUT FOR IN AN INVESTMENT DECISION?

Begin with the end in mind. If you are participating in an innovation competition, what are the judges looking for? If you are working in a corporation and looking for a vice-president to sponsor you, what is he looking for?

The best way to know is to ask.

Lots of senior executives claim to be innovative, but were traditional in their thinking and their decision making. They had not been through an innovation journey before. To understand what makes them tick and open up their wallet, ask them.

If you are taking part in an innovation competition, the decision criteria are usually posted on the website. If not, ask the organizers. Search through the internet to know the past winners and losers. Understand why some contestants won and why some lost. Talk to the winners, talk to the losers, talk to the judges, and learn from their experiences.

LEARNING STEPS

In general, the VISA to sponsorship of your innovation from your management or judges lies in these four common criteria:

► Value / Criticality
► Innovativeness/uniqueness
► Sustainability
► Mass Appeal

To understand how the four criteria can be used to judge how great your innovation is, let's use an analogy of putting food on your dining plate:

► Value is about HOW MUCH MORE food plus the QUALITY of food on your dinner plate

► Innovativeness/uniqueness is about NO ONE OUT THERE eating from your dinner plate

► Sustainability is about HOW LONG MORE your dinner plate will be filled and refilled

► Appeal is about HOW MANY CUSTOMERS will put food onto your dinner plate

Value/Criticality

What added value does your innovation bring to the problem it solves? How critical is your innovation?

How urgent is it?

Does your innovation save lives and limbs?

What are its significant advantages over the existing competing products?

The more critical the problem your innovation solves, the more value it creates. An innovation that prevents cuts and bruises is good, but an innovation that saves lives and limbs is a must-have. In terms of value, customers may be willing to pay $10 extra for an innovation that prevents cuts and bruises, but they are definitely willing to invest thousands of dollars if we can save their limbs or lives. Besides, if your innovation is so great (like car seat belts and air bags), it may be mandated by law.

The same logic works for the degree of importance and urgency. A business traveler who forgot a power adapter for his laptop would not mind paying double or triple the price for the same product. If your innovation fulfills an important or urgent need, then it commands a high value in the eyes of your customer.

Value is about both the tangible and intangible impact. If your innovative machine is faster than the existing ones, we can calculate the dollar value of your speed and its impact to the business. On the other hand, intangible value, like safety, perception, image, branding, and customer satisfaction are difficult to quantify or justify. Properly presented, it can enhance the significance of your innovation.

Where to look for ideas with the most value:

▶ Look around your home, office, and factory. Which is the biggest problem around? What are your colleagues complaining about?

▶ Look into areas that your company can generate the most growth, or save the most amount of money. Which market has the greatest potential for your innovation?

▶ Look into the biggest cost item. Do you have an idea to eliminate or minimize that?

▶ Look into safety issues. Research into the newspaper or web for records of accidents or crisis. Where are the hazardous areas where lives can be saved or injury prevented?

Exciting innovations that sold well immediately after the 911 World Trade Center attack were quick deployment parachutes and stylish skydiving suits for executives to jump off tall buildings in the event of such emergencies.

Jump on critical issues! Leverage on what's hot!

Innovativeness /Uniqueness

In an innovation competition, the degree of innovativeness or uniqueness is very important (it is an innovation contest, remember?). Look out for novelty ideas. It should be something refreshing; something that sparks a "why I didn't think about that" exclamation. Keywords associated with this category that judges are watching out for are uniqueness and originality.

Ask yourself:

▶ What is so special/distinct/original/unique about this idea?
▶ Where is the breakthrough (process/product/technology)?

▶ Is this an original idea or an adaptation of ideas from some other sources?

▶ What is the distinct difference between your innovation and all other existing solutions?

If your answer is a marginal difference or that it does the job better, then your innovation is not innovative enough. A really novel idea is completely different.

Examples of great breakthrough ideas include:

▶ Amazon.com selling books without bookshops

▶ eBay auctions without a middleman, worldwide

▶ Book drop of Singapore National Library eliminating queues completely

▶ eWallet via mobile phone

Contest judges' eyes light up when ideas are truly innovative. Audiences gasped and television viewers were wowed. Such truly innovative ideas are difficult to conceive, to sell, and to implement. It requires the mindset to see things differently, think creatively, and takes guts to challenge the norm. This is what judges are looking for; this is what the competition is about.

Sustainability

Sustainability is the ability of your innovation or the results of your innovation to maintain or increase its value over time. The opposite of a sustainable innovation is called a fad, something that is hot today, forgotten tomorrow. Management does not want to invest in a fad.

A sustainable innovation must be able to produce and retain its value over a long period of time. Sustainability brings in a constant stream of profit far beyond the recovery of its initial investment.

Questions to ask pertaining to sustainability:

▶ Can your innovation be multiplied across different outlets, different regions and into different market segments?

▶ Sustainability is about the life cycle of a product. Does your innovation have a long product life cycle?

▶ Understand each stage of the product life cycle. Can the product life cycle be extended? Be recycled? Be revitalized?

▶ Will there be possible spin-offs?
   ■ From Volume 1 to Volume 2
   ■ From books to CDs to movies
   ■ From movies to action figure toys to electronic games
   ■ From iPod to on-line music stores to accessories

Mass Appeal

A great innovation appeals to millions of people. It must touch everybody's heart and can be used by lots of people. Ideally, it can solve a common problem that affects everybody. The rationale for mass appeal is that there should be more than enough customers to buy your innovation so that you can recover the investment and profit from it.

Some innovations address the needs of a niche market. Mass appeal means that your innovation needs to appeal to the majority in that niche market. If we measure the demand by market share, then your innovation must cause a massive switch from your competitor's products to yours. Products with mass appeal tend to attract word-of-mouth publicity. The product must be well designed, user friendly, stylish, and attractive. Show your innovation to a few potential customers. Talk about it, listen to their feedback. What will attract them to buy?

Products with mass appeal are intuitive. Let your potential customers play with your products. Do they know what the product is without you having to tell them? Do they know how to use it without reading the users' guide?

Questions to ponder:

▶ What is your innovation's impact to your organization, to the industry, and to the society at large?

▶ Does your innovation fulfill a well-defined need that will cause a significant change of behavior from your customer?

▶ Did your customers fall in love with your innovation at first sight? Did they talk about it days later? Did it spread to other customers?

▶ Is the market large/attractive enough to justify the investment of resources and effort for your innovation?

While I advocate Value, Innovativeness, Sustainability, and Appeal as judging criteria, I have seen judges and management using other criteria such as:

▶ Degree of risk
▶ Revenue potential
▶ Minimal investment of resources
▶ Maximum payback or Return on Investment
▶ Ease of implementation
▶ Effectiveness of the solution to solve a certain problem
▶ Alignment to corporate vision, etc

Judging criteria differs greatly depending on what you are judging (consumer products versus industrial products, products versus services or processes). If you are in the management team or judging panel, select what makes most sense for your corporation or to suit your contest objectives.

SELLING YOUR IDEAS

Selling an idea is different from selling a product or a service. There may be multiple stages of selling. Initially, you need to sell the idea to get the first round of funding to build your prototype. Once the prototype is ready, the proof of concept can be tested. You may test the market to some sample customers and fine-tune your prototype to improve it based on the feedback gathered from your sample customers. You will certainly need to sell your ideas again (and again) to secure more funding as you progress along your innovation journey.

What is the difference between selling an innovative idea and selling a product?

When you sell a product or a service, there is something for you to "have and to hold". Products have features, forms, and shapes. Services have well-defined deliverables. There are customer base and reference sites. Potential customers know what they are getting for the money paid.

Selling an innovative idea is like selling vaporware. It is the selling of hopes and dreams. You have nothing to show, no proof that it will work, and no proof that customers will buy. Yet you want the sponsors to open up their wallets.

Because you have nothing to show, you need to inspire them with hopes and dreams. You need to sell the potential that your idea will work and bring in much more money than their investment. You need to convince the sponsor to take calculated risks and that the risks are much smaller than the potential loss of their investment. In other words, you need to appeal to both their mind and their hearts.

UNDERSTANDING THE AUDIENCE

In every competition, there will be a panel of judges. In every corporation, there will be a management team that makes the investment decisions. Before you walk into the presentation room, you need to understand who these decision makers are.

To give contestants and their innovations a fair evaluation, normally you will find a combination of different talents with different experiences within the panel of judges. Who are they and what are their roles?

- ▶ Sponsors, entrepreneurs, and business managers to understand the innovation from the business and financial perspectives
- ▶ Technologists (engineers, scientists, academic professors, etc) to make sure that the innovation is technically feasible
- ▶ Industry experts who understand the industry's norm, competitions, existing products, industry issues, and constraints

Find out if there is a dominant player whose opinion carries the weight of gold. You need to align yourself to his agenda if you hope to see his gold.

Is there a trusted technical advisor within the panel of judges? This is the guy who defines physics in the eyes of decision makers. Make sure you convince him about the technical feasibility of your innovation. It does not matter what Einstein or Isaac Newton said; never argue formulae with this guy during your presentation. Win him over. When he smiles, the law of gravity will pull the gold towards you.

Are there friends and foes within the judging panel? Friends are those that support your innovation. Foes are those that support someone else's innovation over yours. Identify them early. If possible, win them over before the presentation (or at least neutralize the ground).

UNDERSTAND THE ENVIRONMENT

Know your environment.

▶ Go to the presentation venue early to check out the facilities.

▶ What is the meeting room setting?
  ■ Auditorium style, conference room, u-shape table arrangements, cluster seating, etc.

▶ What are the facilities available?
  ■ Do they have a multi-media projector for your notebook?
  ■ Go early to test out the compatibility of your equipment with the conference room equipment. Make sure that your video, animation, and music work.
  ■ Do you need flip-charts and markers?
  ■ Do you need sound systems and CD/DVD players?
  ■ Do they provide wireless microphones?

▶ What is the size of the audience?

▶ Do they have a stage?
  ■ If so, go early. Stand on the stage. Walk around the stage. Feel comfortable with the stage. Imagine yourself speaking to the audience from that stage.
  ■ Test the sound systems. Take note of the position for your clip-microphone to give optimum sound quality and volume.

▶ Is the attire dressing formal or informal?

▶ Do you have props or prototypes to demonstrate?
  ■ If so, who is going to help you set everything up?
  ■ Do you need time and space to set up your props or prototypes?

■ Do you need someone to help you carry them up the stage?

Call the organizers. Let them know your special requirements early.

KNOW YOUR TIMING

A couple of tips about timing:

▶ What is the duration?
   ■ Contest duration usually range from 60 seconds to 10 minutes. This means that you need to be very concise and precise in the presentation of your ideas.
   ■ For such a short duration, you need to rehearse, rehearse, and rehearse until you can make the most impact within the allocated timeframe.
   ■ Some contests rules are strict. The second you exceed the timing, the timer will buzz you out. Prepare your final concluding paragraph well and be prepared to jump into it the moment you get the timeout signal.
   ■ Corporate management presentation usually allows more time to discuss the details, ranging from 30 minutes to one hour.

▶ Which timeslot?
   ■ Are you the first presenter?
     If so, you set the tone for the rest to follow. The judges may not have warmed up yet. Sometimes they may not have even co-ordinated/calibrated their judging criteria. Be cheery and kick-off the event with a great start.
   ■ Are you the eighth, the twelfth, or the last presenter?
     The judges were bored before they even saw you. You need to leave behind something memorable, something exciting, and something that differentiates you from the rest of the crowd.

▶ Do you need time to set up your props?

 ■ If so, request the organizers for a timeslot immediately after the tea-breaks or lunch-breaks. Find out the duration of the break times and use it to your advantage for setting up the props.

 ■ Set up your props early and make use of the remaining break time to socialize with the decision makers.

CONTENT AND STRUCTURE

This is a crucial make or break opportunity for the months or years of effort for the innovator. Within the short span of allocated time, the innovator has to convince the sponsor/judge/management to invest in his dreams. How can you convince the decision makers within just 10 minutes?

1. Open with a grabber

▶ A grabber thrills the sponsors, wakes up the judges, and creates an impact from the moment you articulate your first paragraph. The sponsors want to hear what's so great about your innovation. Give it to them and wow them in your first paragraph.

"Stone Age did not end when we ran out of stones,
Bronze Age did not end when we ran out of bronze,
Our Oil Age will not end when we ran out of oil,
Tomorrow, with our innovation, we shall end the Oil Age"[52]
Wow!

▶ Use a teaser. Say something that will make your audience thirsty for more. One of the great presentations I had heard began with:

---

[52] This script had been taken from the book by Canton, James (2007) The Extreme Future: The Top Trends that will reshape the world in the next 20 years. Penguin Group.

"I love flying. Last year, I flew 18 times and landed six times with the plane."

He paused, leaving the audience wondering what happened to the other 12 times. The presenter proceeded with the rest of his presentation and we learnt that he was a paratrooper. He jumped off the plane the remaining times.

▶ Begin with the headline. Think of what the headline in tomorrow's newspaper will be if your innovation is wildly successful. Headlining is a powerful technique that brings your sponsors into the future world when your innovation conquers the world.

2. Highlight the issues
▶ Having caught the sponsor's attention, this is the time to proceed to the body of your presentation.
▶ Highlight what problems your innovations are trying to solve.
▶ Stress the severity of the problems.
▶ Illustrate what the nightmare will be if the problems are not solved.
▶ Substantiate with statistics, records, or data gathered.
▶ Use simple language, avoiding any technical 'jargon' that the audience may be unfamiliar with.

3. Explain your innovation
▶ This is the moment of truth when you explain what your innovation is about, how great it is, the value that it contributes, and the great difference between your solution and all the other existing solutions.
▶ If possible, illustrate the "before" and "after" picture vividly so that the judges can see the dramatic differences your innovation makes. Employ film video clips of people trying to solve the problem with and without using your innovation. Show the big difference.
▶ Build up your case, use data of the value your innovation contributes.

▶ Demonstrate your prototype live in front of the judges. Show that it works.

▶ Show how happy/satisfied your customers were while using or after using your innovation. Show how easy it is for kids (or grandmothers) to use your products.

▶ Cite examples, situations, scenarios where your innovations can be applied. Select a few impactful scenarios.

▶ Use metaphors, analogies, stories to illustrate points.

4. Call for action

▶ End your presentation with a call for action.

▶ Stress the urgency for them to approve/sponsor your innovation.

▶ Reiterate your main points.

▶ Leave your audience with something memorable. Remember, there are many presenters before and after your presentation. What key points do you want them to remember the morning after?

Tips for Successful Presentation

▶ Present important stuff first. Be flexible with timing (you may be asked to shorten your presentation because the previous speaker eats into your time!)

▶ Ask a few leading questions to where you want the final close to be, like:

   ■ Is it important that we must act now to save innocent lives from drunk driving?

   ■ Do you agree that every man, woman, and child should have access to clean cheap water?

▶ Judges and sponsors like to critic and give their comments (it's their job!). Be open to comments and suggestions. Do not be defensive. Judges and sponsors mean well. Adopt a learning attitude to their feedback. Just say, "Thank you, I shall take note of that."

DIFFERENTIATING WINNERS FROM LOSERS

Let's take some real life cases to illustrate. We shall examine the winners of the American Inventors for Season 1 (2006) and Season 2 (2007) using the Value, Innovativeness, Sustainability, Appeal (VISA) as our judging criteria.

Season 1: Anecia Safety Capsule

In Season 1 of the popular American Inventor[53] series 2006, the winner of the million dollar prize was Janusz Liberkowski[54] . Janusz invented a new type of child safety car seat based on the human womb and called the Anecia Safety Capsule[55] . It is shaped like a sphere with a movable sphere inside it. In the event of a car accident, the sphere will move, lessening the force on the baby.

VALUE

▶ The Anecia Safety Capsule could save the life of your baby! What could be more valuable and powerful than that? It grabbed the attention of the judges and TV viewers immediately.

▶ During the show, the inventor Janusz showed a video clip of a dramatic car crash and a hysterical woman outside screaming, "My baby! My baby!" She rushed into scene and flung open the door of the wrecked car. The audience held their breath as the camera zoomed into the interior of the smoky car to reveal the face of a smiling baby, safe, and sound.

▶ Life is priceless. This invention touched every heart and mind.

---

53 http://en.wikipedia.org/wiki/Americian Inventor. (2006).

54 http://en.wikipedia.org/wiki/Janusz_Liberkowski

55 http://inventorspot.com/update_on_the_anecia_survival_casule

INNOVATIVENESS

▶ When a car crashes, there are two collisions. The first collision occurs when the car hits the other car or obstacle. The second collision is when the baby is squashed against the seat belt or when the baby's head and neck are snapped in the direction of the impact, at the same speed that the car was going before the crash. The whipping action of the child's head and the forces on the head and neck structure during any impact are the main causes of child fatality.

▶ Traditional car seats are designed to try and hold the child with little or poor support for the head and neck. In the crash test, it was calculated that at 30 miles per hour, the force on the baby's neck is 74 lbs for a classic car seat and just 8 lbs for the Anecia Safety Capsule. This was the proven supporting data that greatly differentiated the winning invention from the existing solutions.

▶ The innovativeness came from the design of the swivel base in the Anecia Safety Capsule. It protects the baby from crashes from all directions. When the force hits, the baby instantly shifts. The force is absorbed, as the baby is rotated perpendicular to the impact force. And, most importantly, if the car spins, bounces, or is hit more than once, the seat automatically adapts in less than 0.005 seconds to align and protect the baby. No matter what direction the hit is from, the baby's head and neck are always supported. This fact once again vastly differentiated the invention from traditional car seats.

SUSTAINABILITY

▶ Noting that this Anecia Safety Capsule is designed to protect infants from birth to seven months of age, the usage life-cycle is short.

▶ To counter this short life-cycle, the inventor and the manufacturer were exploring rental as their marketing strategy. At the time of writing this book, the product is under development with Evenflo, a maker of baby care products.

▶ Millions of families have children. Once this innovation hits the market, the sustainability goes on forever.

APPEAL

▶ The invention is attractively designed and can be fitted into 95% of normal car seats. It has an inner basket, containing the baby, which can be easily removed and fit into an optional stroller, without waking up the baby.

▶ Isn't this a wow? The inventor had pictured how a customer is likely to use the innovation in their daily life and had anticipated the various problems. He had the design well thought out, incorporating the ease of use. It has all the elements of a sure winner.

▶ Once again, this innovation reaches out to every family. The mass appeal potential is huge.

Season 2: Guardian Angel

In Season 2[56] (2007), firefighter Greg Chavez[57] , who invented the fire suppression system for Christmas trees, was declared the champion. His invention comprised of a small, pressurized tank of water, disguised as a Christmas package, which is placed under the Christmas tree. It is attached to a small hose leading to the top of the tree where a fusible link is disguised as an angel. If the Christmas tree catches fire, the heat from the fire triggers the link and water suppresses the fire. There is also an alarm that sounds to get people out of the house alive.

Let's examine what's so good about his invention and why it captured the hearts of the judges and the audience.

---

[56] http://en.wikipedia.org/wiki/Americian Inventor. (2007).

[57] http://en.wikipedia.org/wiki/Greg_Chavez

VALUE

▶ During his presentation, Greg told a touching story about an incident that inspired him to create the Guardian Angel. He recalled a man dashing out from a burning house with the lifeless body of his daughter. That man lost his child and his home because of a Christmas tree fire. His haunting story was a grabber that brought tears into the judges' eyes.

▶ He proceeded to show a video clip on how a tiny spark from faulty Christmas lights or a short circuit could ignite the Christmas tree. Within less than nine seconds, the entire Christmas tree was engulfed in flames. The speed of fire shocked the audience and reinforced the real danger of families being burnt alive if Christmas trees fires were not detected and extinguished within seconds.

▶ Greg had cleverly presented the before and after scenarios, illustrating the horror without his innovation, and the workability of his innovation to suppress the fire, giving the family time to run out of the house and get help.

▶ Once again, the value of this innovation is priceless; it saves human lives.

INNOVATIVENESS

▶ Greg's invention was unique. He had discovered the problem as part of his job as a fireman and had created the awareness of Christmas tree fires.

▶ Greg had discovered a niche market that was not addressed by any existing products. Fire engulfed the Christmas tree and set the entire living room on fire within nine seconds. The time is too short for anyone to reach for a fire extinguisher, or even to evacuate family members. In a niche market, he has no competition.

SUSTAINABILITY

▶ Christmases are evergreen (or ever-white). It recurs forever. This means that once the Guardian Angel establishes itself as a must-have for Christmas, the sustainability extends year after year.

APPEAL

▶ Greg cleverly blended his innovation into its natural environment by disguising the water tank to look like a gift under the Christmas tree and the fusible link, disguised as the guardian angel, which naturally sits on top of Christmas trees.

▶ The innovation looks lovely and fits into the 'must-have' for every home.

▶ Greg's fireman attire and status brought the judges and audience closer to him as he is portrayed as an average working American, leveraging on the image of firemen as heroes since the 911 attack. If Greg had a PhD or was an engineer working in a multinational corporation, the appeal would not be as powerful.

Having learnt what differentiates a winner from the other mediocre innovations, is your innovation clearly outstanding? How does your innovation fare when benchmarked against the VISA criteria?

Take time to improve and to fine-tune. Make yours an award-winning innovation.

Leave behind a legacy!

SUMMARY

Summary Notes

1. To recap what we discussed earlier, judge your innovation using VISA criteria:
    a. Value is about HOW MUCH MORE food plus the QUALITY of food on your dinner plate
    b. Innovativeness/uniqueness is about NO ONE OUT THERE eating from your dinner plate
    c. Sustainability is about HOW LONG MORE your dinner plate will be filled and refilled
    d. Appeal is about HOW MANY CUSTOMERS will put food onto your dinner plate

2. Preparation to sell your ideas:
    a. Understand the audience
    b. Know the environment
    c. Know your timing

3. Content and Structure of your presentation
    a. Begin with a grabber
    b. Highlight the issues
    c. Explain your innovation
    d. Call for action

CHAPTER 10
IMPLEMENTATION

"Quick, let's implement it before our competitors
realise that we stole their idea."

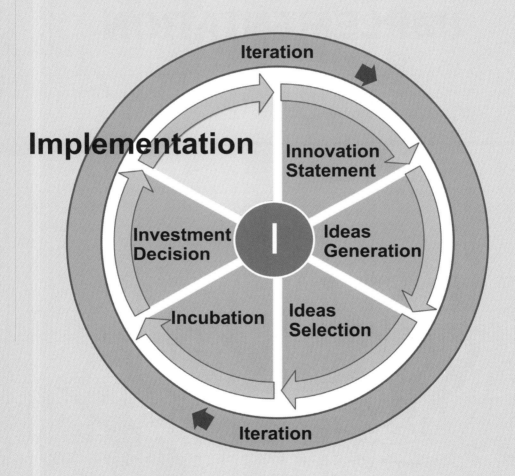

CHAPTER 10: IMPLEMENTATION

Having convinced your management and secured the funding, you can now embark on the detailed implementation of your innovation. It is time to turn your ideas into gold.

It is not my intention to cover in detail how to implement innovation as a project. However, I found that over 90% of the participants in my innovation workshops critically lack both the skills and experience of project management. In this chapter, I'd like to give you an essential outline on project management, and I'd like to concentrate on specific areas pertaining to the implementation of innovation projects.

For full methodology and best practices[58] [59] [60] about project implementation, I strongly encourage readers and project leaders to refer to the library of project management books available in the market. As the Innovation Team Leader usually performs the role of a Project Manager, I shall use both terms interchangeably.

IMPLEMENTING INNOVATION AS A PROJECT

A project is defined as a temporary endeavor undertaken to create a unique product or service or result. Projects are **temporary** as there is a definite beginning and a definite end result that the project will accomplish. It is **unique** in terms of its deliverables. This definition fits perfectly into an innovation project as all innovations are unique in some form, shape, or deliverables.

A project is a carefully defined set of activities that uses resources (money, people, materials, energy, space, provisions, communication,

---

[58] Project Management Institute. (2004). Guide to the Project Management Body of Knowledge. http://www.pmi.org/

[59] Projects in Controlled Environment PRINCE2, http://www.ogc.gov.uk/prince2/

[60] The International Project Management Association, http://www.ipma.ch/

motivation, etc) to achieve the project goals and objectives. It has a life cycle comprising of Initiating, Planning, Executing, Controlling and Monitoring, and Closing phases.

A good project manager seeks to achieve all of the project goals and objectives within the project constraints of scope, time, and budget.

In many companies, the Innovation Project Implementation Team is separated from the Innovation Ideas Generation Team. This is done deliberately so that the Ideas Generation Team is not inhibited by their lack of skills, implementation experience, or resources constraints. If the Ideas Generator is also the Ideas Implementer, then the disadvantage is that the ideas generated tend to be more implementable. Few out-of-the-box ideas may emerge.

TRADITIONAL PROJECT MANAGEMENT VERSUS INNOVATION PROJECT MANAGEMENT

What is the difference between traditional project management and innovation project management?

A traditional project that focuses on enhancement or improvement effort of an existing environment cannot be considered as an innovation project. The end result may be marginally better and is not a quantum leap from its existing status. As an example, a Six Sigma project that improves the consistency of a service from 98% to 99% and then to 99.999% reliability makes use of several problem solving techniques. The bulk of the effect focuses on removing errors and reworks. Such a project is about perfecting a process. This cannot be considered an innovation project as it does not involve innovative techniques.

An innovation project involves doing things uniquely different like inventing a new product or eliminating the entire processes all together or reshuffling the sequencing of processes within a service. The results are dramatically different from status quo or mere improvements.

Innovation can trigger a project. It can create a new product or it can destroy the entire industry. If innovation can generate ideas that make a process redundant, then why bother doing a Six Sigma to perfect a redundant process? This means that innovation is Step Zero in project management. Innovation techniques can be used BEFORE the implementation phase of a project as well as DURING and WITHIN each phase of project management.

An Innovation Project team:

▶ Begins with the definition and the reframing of the Innovation Statement
▶ Brainstorms thousands of possible ideas during the Idea Generation phase
▶ Systematically sorts out the thousands into the best few selected ideas based on the perspective-criteria matrix
▶ Incubates the selected ideas to enhance and to make the ideas more practical
▶ Presents to the sponsor or management for investment decision
▶ Once the go-ahead approval has been given, the Implementation Project Management begins

Using innovation techniques prior to implementing a traditional project management ensures that all possible ideas are explored and that only the best possible ideas are selected and implemented.

PHASES OF A PROJECT

Initiation of a project:

▶ This is equivalent to the Investment Decision phase of the Innovation cycle. At this stage, the innovation project is authorized by the sponsor, the scope is defined, and the budgets and resources are allocated.

PROJECT PLANNING

Learning Steps

LEARNING STEPS

Project planning is a vital phase in project management. All projects are built twice, once in the plan and once on the actual ground. With proper planning, mega-skyscrapers can stand tall even before the first brick is laid. Planning guides the entire project execution, eliminates uncertainty and risks, and forms a basis for monitoring and controlling. The various activities involved in planning are:

▶ Scope definition
   ■ Documents the project scope details with clear specifications, outlining the major deliverables, the assumptions and constraints. It also states the boundaries of what is and is not within the coverage of the project.
   ■ Innovation Technique: Reframing
     ⇨ Is the scope too restrictive for further innovative ideas to emerge during the implementation?
     ⇨ Which constraints are necessary and which are not?
     ⇨ Which specifications are critical and which are not?
     ⇨ Let's do some reframing of the project scope and innovation statement to explore if we can find a better scope.
▶ Activity definition
   ■ Defines the specific activities that need to be performed to produce the various project deliverables. It makes use of tools and techniques to decompose activities into smaller chunks of work packages. These work packages can be scheduled with estimates of expertise, time, materials, and budget needed.

- The output of activity definition is in activity lists, activities attributes, and milestones.
- Innovation Technique: SCAMPER
  - ⇨ Brainstorm using SCAMPER technique: Can any of the activities be combined?
  - ⇨ If we eliminate one of the activities block, how can we still achieve the objectives?

▶ Sequencing
  - Defines and documents dependencies among scheduled activities
  - Activities are scheduled in logical sequence with precedence relationships so as to understand the leads and lags of each activity and how they support the later development of a realistic and achievable project schedule.
  - Innovation Technique: SCAMPER
    - ⇨ Try rearranging the sequencing. Which sequence can work better?
    - ⇨ If possible, try getting a different team to plan in Reverse sequence (plan the last step first). Compare this with the sequencing plan from the first step. Where are the differences? Choose the better sequence or adapt the best of both.
    - ⇨ Which are the most critical bottlenecks in your sequencing?
    - ⇨ Brainstorm what are the ways to ensure that the bottlenecks do not jeopardize the entire project.
    - ⇨ Brainstorm the different ways to bypass the bottlenecks.

▶ Resources planning
  - This is the process of estimating:
    - ⇨ What resources (people, expertise, equipment,

infrastructure, material, etc)?
- ⇨ How much resources are required to perform each scheduled activity?
- ⇨ When are such resources needed to perform each of the activities?
- ■ For Human Resource Planning, we need to:
  - ⇨ Identify and document the project and project members' roles, responsibilities, authorities, and reporting relationships.
  - ⇨ Identify and maintain an expertise-competency matrix so that we can assign the right task to the right person.
- ■ Innovation technique: SCAMPER
  - ⇨ Which critical resources are being tied up for extended periods of time? Try "<u>Put to other use</u>" other resources, which can perform the same tasks in a different way.
  - ⇨ Try <u>simplification</u>. Are there activities that can be simplified? Can any of the steps be <u>minimized</u>?

► Cost estimate/budgeting
- ■ Production of a budget necessary to fund the various activities in the project: Understand the various cost elements, how money will be spent, and when the money needs to be available.
- ■ Cost estimate should extend across the innovation's life cycle, which includes the cost of creating, developing, building, testing, installing, using, maintaining, supporting, and retiring the product or service.
- ■ Innovation Technique: SCAMPER
  - ⇨ Which are your most expensive resources? Brainstorm using "Substitute" to explore cheaper alternatives.
  - ⇨ Brainstorm the different ways to minimize the use of expensive resources.

⇨ How can we modify the plan to save cost?

▶ Quality planning

- ■ Quality is planned, designed, and built into the project and not as an aftereffect of the project. Quality planning identifies which quality standards are necessary and relevant for the project.

- ■ Quality comes with cost. The benefit-cost analysis balances the optimal level of quality with the appropriate investment in cost for the project.

- ■ Innovation Technique: Perspective-Criteria Matrix

  ⇨ In the selection of ideas, include quality and cost as part of the idea selection criteria. Which are the best ideas balancing quality and cost?

▶ Risk identification and management

- ■ Identify the probable risks that might affect the project and documenting their characteristics.

  ⇨ Assign probable risk owners.

  ⇨ Decide on risk probability and impact.

  ⇨ Identify appropriate counter-action to mitigate the identified risks.

- ■ Innovation Technique: Perspective-Criteria Matrix/PENS

  ⇨ Which ideas balance the best results with the minimum risks?

  ⇨ Which minimal actions do we need to mitigate the risks?

  ⇨ How can I remove the risks using the P.E.N.S. technique?

PROJECT EXECUTION

Execution is the phase that does the actual work defined in the project management plan. The output of planning phase is a sequenced and structured set of work packages detailing what to do, who does what, and when. Team members are assigned to execute the work packages with assigned resources.

Each work package consists of a small chunk of work activities, which can be independently defined, scheduled, and managed. A technique used in project management is to arrange these work packages into a deliverable-oriented hierarchical manner called a Work Breakdown Structure (WBS)[61] . A WBS can be decomposed into finer level of details as it does down the hierarchical. It provides a common framework for the development of the overall planning and control of the project.

The project manager is the main driving force behind the execution phase. He coordinates people and resources, manages time, schedules, costs, and risks. He ensures that the execution of each work packages happens and produces quality outputs in accordance to the plan. Throughout the journey, he provides the leadership and takes corrective actions where necessary to steer the project back on course.

CRITICAL SUCCESS FACTORS

Implementing an innovative project is like treading on untrodden snow. You stand alone in the wilderness without a single footprint to follow. No one has been here before. How can you proceed?

Cautiously of course! To reach your destination, you need to know what and where your major obstacles are. Identify these obstacles as early in your planning and implementation cycle as possible. If you have to cross

---

[61] http://www.pmi.org/ The Project Management Institute

rivers, make sure you have boats. If you need to cross crevasses, make sure you carry ladders and ropes. You do not wait till you reach the river banks before you realize that you need boats.

I called these major obstacles, road-blocks, show-stoppers our critical success factors (CSF). These are critical elements that are vital to the success of our project.

Caution!

▶ **What are your critical success factors that will determine or undermine your success?**

▶ **Is it a core research breakthrough you are depending on?**

▶ **Is it customer acceptance of your new product?**

▶ **Or is it the speed of product development?**

Whatever you have determined as your critical success factors, make very sure you are able to attain them. Invest maximum resources and energy to make sure that your key success factors do not slip or fail.

How can you ensure that your CSF comes true?

If your CSF is the funding from a major customer, then figure out a way to the funding commitment first before you begin detailed work.

Let's assume that your CSF is the breakthrough of a certain new technology. Instead of waiting for the breakthrough to happen (or fail), brainstorm what is the quickest and cheapest way to produce the proof of concept. The proof of concept is a short, incomplete way to prove that the idea or concept works. Remember that a mountain climber does not need to build bridges to cross the crevasses; he simply uses an improvised wobbly ladder.

PROTOTYPING

Powerful Quotes

"I've always had a feeling that any time you can experiment, you ought to do it. Because you never know what will happen."

- Walt Disney

What can you do, quickly and cheaply, to demonstrate the feasibility of your idea or the theoretical principle behind the idea?

Building the full design is expensive and can be time-consuming, especially when several iterations are necessary – building the full design, figuring out what the problems are and how to solve them, then building another full design. Prototyping is a good and cheap way to test the proof of your concept.

There are various ways you can do prototyping. You can

▶ Build a smaller scaled-down version or model:

- ■ As in a building design, automobile, landscaping, etc
  - ⇨ To illustrate your concept and ideas
  - ⇨ To help you communicate with sponsors, users, customers
  - ⇨ To garner feedback on the design for modification or enhancement
- ■ Innovation Technique: Brainstorm <u>Minimize</u>
  - ⇨ Which critical part of my innovation do I need to prototype and test?
  - ⇨ How can I minimize the prototype to the bare minimum and yet be able to test and prove the concept of my innovation?

▶ Build it partially
- As in mechanical design or computer programming:
  ⇨ To prove that the critical components work
  ⇨ To understand the dynamics of critical parts in motion with relation to each other
  ⇨ To simulate the workings of a bigger machine/system
  ⇨ To figure out the technical logic
  ⇨ To solve the complexity of the design
  ⇨ To ensure that the interfacing with other bigger systems work
- Innovation Technique:
  ⇨ Isolate the components within a sub-unit that needs to be tested and provide it the basic parameters or inputs so that the sub-unit can function independently.
  ⇨ Perform the various tests to prove that each critical sub-unit works independently.
  ⇨ Assemble the sub-units into bigger building blocks and test their interactions and dynamics.

▶ Build it with cheaper material
- As in product design or manufacturing:
  ⇨ To confirm the design with customers before manufacturing with actual expensive material
  ⇨ To test out different designs cheaply (test and throw)
  ⇨ To test the different types of possible materials for the actual product before mass production
- Innovation Technique: Brainstorm <u>Substitute</u>
  ⇨ Which part/material is the most expensive?
  ⇨ Which characteristics in the expensive materials are essential to the final product? Why are these materials so expensive?
  ⇨ What cheaper materials can I substitute it with, yet retain these essential characteristics?

▶ Build on different materials
- As in visual design and product marketing:

⇨ To solicit inputs regarding various designs, forms, sizes, and materials from customers

⇨ To try out different colors, texture, shades or features in the market before the launch of the actual product

■ Innovation Technique: Focus on the customers

⇨ If the customer's inputs on the look-and-feel are important, get them early.

⇨ Understand what's important and valuable to the customers.

⇨ Understand what's not important or valuable to the customers.

⇨ Use different materials that can amplify what is valuable and save on what is not valuable to the customers.

▶ Build on simulated platform

■ Before building the big actual machine, like the Boeing 787 Dreamliner

⇨ Simulate the entire Boeing in the computer system.

⇨ Solving technical problems in the design using computer is easier, faster, and cheaper than using the real mechanical and hydraulic parts.

⇨ Shapes and sizes of inter-related parts can be modified with the click of a mouse.

⇨ Prove that the design works before the actual full construction of the plane.

Using prototypes, we can quickly and cheaply filter out designs that do not work before the building of more expensive full systems or before the mass production of actual products. Solving and sorting out the technical complexities through prototypes will boost the confidence of the project team and minimize the risk of failure down the road.

Testing is the next essential stage. It is generally performed by a combination of technical testers and end users, and can occur after the prototype is built or concurrently. Controls should be in place to ensure that the final product will meet the specifications of the project objectives.

The results should show that both the prototype, and later the actual product:

► Meet the objectives of the Innovation Statement
► Satisfies the business and customers requirements
► Performs the functionality as designed
► Can achieve the specified quality standards (e.g. reliability)
► Can be produced within time and budget constraints

RISK MANAGEMENT

When we innovate, we explore a brand new frontier. In the wilderness, there is always unseen danger and there is always the incomprehensible unknown. The more innovative your project is, the further your ship sails away from the coastline, the bigger the risk.

In innovation, risk management is vital if you want your innovation to bear fruits. I have seen many perfectly sound innovative ideas gone to waste when risks were not managed upfront or in time. I have also seen innovative projects being cancelled at the slightest hint of a foreseeable risk. The difference between an innovation that bears fruit and one that wastes time is proper risk management.

Risk is any event or condition that may cause your project to fail. Risks are everywhere, and can occur when you least expect. Examples of risks include:

► Unavailability or lack of funds, resources, expertise or money
► Unexpected accidents to key infrastructures or personnel
► Breakdown of main systems or key components
► Unexpected delay of equipment, development or logistics
► Human related risks, like resignation, sickness or low morale
► Competitors' actions and reactions
► Changes in trends, industry, economic or market conditions
► Disasters like fire, typhoon or floods

Specific to innovation projects, additional risks include the unavailability of knowledge and expertise, unproven new technology, unfamiliarity with new products, resistance to change, and uncertainty of new product acceptance by customers, users, and the market. The combination of the probability of occurrences of the above risks can be quite significant.

Risk Management is the process and activities that focus on assessing, mitigating, and monitoring risks to maximize the chances of project success. A good project manager should anticipate, prevent and proactively manage risks. Risk management consists of the following phases:

► Identification of risks
- List the top five most possible risks pertaining to the innovation project

► Assess the identified risks for
- Their potential severity of loss of assets value or financial impact
- strength of possible threats
- Own vulnerability and weaknesses
- The probability of occurrence

► Using risk assessment information, we can prioritize the risk and decide on what counteractions to take to mitigate risks.

► Possible techniques to mitigate risks are:
- Risk Avoidance
  ⇨ Selecting ideas where solutions/technologies/market segments that are proven
  ⇨ Selecting the proven methodology to avoid risks
  ⇨ Balance the avoidance of risk with the missing out of the opportunities for such innovations
- Risk Reduction
  ⇨ Prototyping the critical portion of your innovation early reduces the risk as critical technologies are already tested

in a smaller scale and prior to the building of the major system.

⇨ Prototyping reduces risks as feedback and acceptance are obtained from potential customers prior to mass production.

■ Risk Transference

⇨ By outsourcing a portion of the project to third parties who have better competency or expertise on specific areas of the innovation than your own.

■ Risk Acceptance

⇨ Accept that some risks do exist and budget for contingency and insurance expenses.

OPPORTUNITY MANAGEMENT

Risks can be either positive or negative. Events, conditions, and situations may either work towards our favor or against us. While project management professionals called them positive and negative risks, I shall term the positive risks as opportunities.

Through our innovation project, we need to pay attention to changing conditions and situations that may result as emerging opportunities for our project. Once opportunity strikes, we can select our course of action:

▶ Exploit

■ A new technology or product is now available in the market. Instead of building our own, we can exploit it by buying the technology to integrate into our project.

■ A new market has opened up; we can exploit the situation by focusing our innovation on the new market instead.

▶ Enhance

■ Computer hardware price has dropped. Enhance this opportunity by increasing the use of computer technologies to increase the chance of success for the project.

▶ Share
  ■ You found a vendor or subcontractor who is capable of or has the expertise to fulfill part of the innovation project. Form a partnership/joint venture with him or share the benefits/value with him.
▶ Accept
  ■ Make a conscious decision not to take any action to leverage on this opportunity, probably because the opportunity is not aligned with the overall strategy.

CHANGE MANAGEMENT AND CONTROL

There are two types of change:

▶ Changes (internal and external) to the project scope, objectives, deliverables, work packages, etc
▶ People behavioral changes as the result of the innovation

PROJECT RELATED CHANGES

From the commencement of the innovation project to the completion and delivery of the innovative product, the time duration may range from a few months to several years. During this period, many changes could have taken place. Some of the changes are external forces (competition actions, economic situation, customers' preference, trends, etc), while others are internal driven. Internal driven changes are often triggered as a result of or as a response to the external driven changes, such as:

▶ Changes in business direction affecting the alignment with the project
▶ Enhancement of scope, upsetting the entire project plan

▶ Project objectives, causing a relook at the relevance to some of the work activities and resources

▶ Personnel resignation, transferring in or out of the project team

▶ Addition, subtraction or modification of product /services features, etc

To ensure project control, such internal driven changes need to be:

1. Formally submitted to the project manager. Each change request needs to be identified (numbered) and tracked.

2. Assessed by a Change Advisory Board[62][63] . This is a team, comprising of the project manager, the sponsor, and the representatives of stakeholders, formed to evaluate the impact of the change.

3. Based on the recommendation by the Change Advisory Board, the project manager can approve or reject the change request.

4. If approved, the change need to be scheduled in the plan and resources need to be allocated to implement the change.

5. Change can therefore be managed and tracked in a controlled manner.

PEOPLE BEHAVIORAL CHANGE

Everybody loves to change to a new car, but nobody like to change the way they drive a car. Imagine if the steering wheel is replaced with a joystick and the pedals are all in different positions; we will protest and complain about the difficulty and the user-unfriendliness of driving the new car. We probably will not buy such cars with the gear stick and pedal in different positions. Humans love changes, but we are resistance to changing our behavior.

---

[62] http://www.best-management-practice.com/IT-Service-Management-ITIL/

[63] http://www.itil-officialsite.com/home/home.asp

To innovate is to change; the more dramatic your innovation is, the greater the resistance you will encounter. A good innovation project leader needs to learn how to manage change effectively. Let's take a look at the following scenario:

You are an IT manager in Automotive Assembly Company (AA) and you have a great idea of a brand new system that will revolutionize the world, or at least your office. You are all charged up to go to the moon. More realistically, you are all set to embark on a new course of actions towards a dream mission of transforming AA to be the most efficient company in the entire automotive industry. You look around and you soon realize that you are surrounded by hundreds, if not thousands, of employees who are happily doing the things they are doing today.

Perhaps you need not look that far. Just look at your opposite cubicle or the manager sitting next to you. Michael is busy doing a lot of things. He is a hardworking guy and a perfectionist. He double-checks and triple-checks his invoices before sending them out. Much of Michael's work will be obsolete once your breakthrough innovation is implemented. How are you going to convince the management team, including Michael, to embark on the innovation journey with you, even if it is for the betterment of your organization?

You get out of your cubicle and stroll down the aisle leading to the water cooler. Along the way, you notice that many of your other colleagues are also busy doing things that do not make sense once your breakthrough innovation is in place. Will they accept your innovation? Will they resist and rebel? How are they going to cope with the changes you are about to introduce?

You meet Peter at the water cooler. Peter has been with the company many years before you. He is well respected as someone who is competent with his work and his customers. If fact, some may say Peter is a walking encyclopedia. He can rattle off seven-digit automotive part numbers off the top of his head and knows which supplier to call when a customer orders an obsolete product. How are you going to convince Peter that your innovation is far more superior and that Peter can forget all the seven-digit part numbers now?

Whether it is a grand Mt. Everest plan, a breakthrough process, or even a simple shortcut to a more efficient system, people are going to resist changes. The secret to getting support for your breakthrough idea is through both the heart and the mind. The secret to successful breakthrough implementation is through proper **Change Management**.

Behavioral change management is concerned with managing the expectations of people at all levels of the organization that are affected by your innovation project and preparing them for the changes they are about to experience so that the project goes smoothly. Your innovation may obsolete their skills, needing them to change the way they think and work. Change management provides them with adequate support and new skills development as their roles change. The better change is managed in one project, the better people will be able to deal with the next change coming down the line. When it is well managed, it helps to implement our innovation for today so that we can achieve our vision of tomorrow. Implementation of innovation change management applies to individuals, work groups, organizational levels, and organizations as a whole.

When we introduce innovation, we introduce change. The more innovative your project is, the more drastic the change will be. Change management, from the people's perspective is therefore vital to the acceptance of your new innovation.

It is vital to ensure that change is properly managed so that people involved in the change are able and willing to adopt the new processes, systems, technologies, skills, organizational structures, behaviors, attitudes, or other changes to lower the risk associated with the project. Even if there are people who are adaptable to change quickly, it is also important to communicate to them the reason for change and the benefits that can arise from the change so that everyone is able to perform to their maximum potential and capability. You also need the entire team dynamics and committed to the change, so it is important to get the team steered towards the goal.

So we are talking about handling both innovation project management (making sure that innovation itself is successful) and change management (making sure that people affected by the innovation accept it) to ensure project success. This certainly sounds like common sense but (a significant but) most programs fail to deliver what they set out to deliver. Why do programs fail? Most barriers are people related and unsurprisingly most enablers are also people related. People make or break change. Therefore it is critical to involve them right at the beginning of the project.

Change management is a process that involves continuity and people. People's attitudes toward change follow a predictable pattern, but their attitudes and perceptions can be very different at different points in the project. Different people will be at different points on the curve as well. People may go through the pattern many times during the same change. When time gets pressured it is easy to assume that people – from sponsors to individuals in a particular department – will do what you need. They won't! People are a whole lot more difficult to manage in a change project. People might not agree with the change, not think they have the right skills, or be keen to maintain existing silo mentalities. It is therefore important to recognize that change does not and cannot happen overnight.

Back to our fictitious Automotive Assembly Company, both Michael and Peter will be scared to death of your innovation project. They will feel that all their decades of experience came to a squeaking halt as they felt themselves being replaced by your more efficient computer systems. Nope, you will not get their cooperation, unless, of course, the change management is properly executed.

It is very important to tackle resistance to change properly. When faced with resistance, remember the following:

▶ People (like Peter and Michael) have to understand 'what's in it for me' and 'why the change'.
▶ What's the new role for people like Peter and Michael? They need to be trained on the new skills.
▶ No surprises: Most people instinctively resist change when they are caught off their guard.

► Nothing changes unless behavior changes.

► Behavior can be changed and attitude will follow or vice versa.

► Allow people to talk about their doubts, fears, and disagreements.

► Clarify expectations; most people want to do what is expected of them.

► Involve the people affected by the change in creating the solution.

Management has an important role to play in managing the change resistance. Some actions that managers and senior executives can take to manage resistance are:

► Hold periodic big team meetings for those affected by the changes.

► Be readily accessible to individuals and groups in the organization to discuss issues. Be visible and actively involved in the change effort.

► Take bold action where warranted in support of the change effort's goals.

► Reward participation in and support of the change effort.

► Align the organization's systems and structures to support the new strategic direction.

THE ROCKET SCIENCE OF LOW-COST AIRLINES

To create the maximum impact, corporate-wide innovations should be implemented such that the different projects complement each other and are all aligned to the corporate vision and business objectives. Let's explore how reinforcing innovations had changed the world of aviations that enabled the budget airlines (new entrants) to send shockwaves down the giants' spines.

The concept of the budget airline[64] was pioneered by Pacific Southwest Airlines in the United States since 1949. Thereafter, the concept spread

---

[64] http://en.wikipedia.org/wiki/Budget_airline

across United States, Europe then to Asia. Some of the most successful airlines include Southwest Airlines[65] in the United States and Ireland's Ryanair[66] . Differentiating itself from the full service traditional airlines (such as the Singapore Airlines, British Airways, etc), a budget airline offers a no-frills, minimum service, low fare flight to passengers.

What makes budget airlines successful?

How can such budget airlines remain profitable (and sometimes even more profitable than traditional full service airlines) after giving such a hefty discount off the traditional airfare?

The success and proliferation of budget airlines around the world was due to the **Business Strategy Innovations**. Taking each of the frills offered by a full service airline, ask the following:

▶ How much does it cost us to provide this frill?
▶ How much value do customers want to pay for this frill?
▶ How does each of the values reinforce or counter each other?

The idea is to create maximum value with the minimum cost, thereby maximizing profit and customer satisfaction.

Let's look at what's so innovative about the budget airline business model.

1. The main key to the success was their ability to turn around the aircraft in 25 minutes instead of 45 minutes or an hour. As most budget airlines operate short haul flights, faster turnaround time means that they are able to get one to two more flights per day per aircraft. More time in the air means more revenue per aircraft.

2. Contributing to and supporting the fast turnaround strategy, the airlines:

    a. Do not serve hot meals. No hot meals translate to the advantage

---

65 http://www.southwest.com/

66 http://www.ryanair.com/

of no need to load and unload hot meals, no clearing of plates, cleaning of spillages, etc).

b. Do not transfer luggage. No unnecessary waiting time or charges.

3. No business class was offered. It makes sense as their target customers are budget travelers, meaning single passenger class flight.

a. Maximizes the seating capacity
b. Means a simple fare scheme, such as charging one-way tickets half that of round-trips (typically fares increase as the plane fills up, which rewards early reservations)
c. Facilitates the strategy of unreserved seating and encourages passengers to board early and quickly

4. A single type of airplane (commonly the Airbus A319 or Boeing 737), reducing training costs, servicing costs, and logistics spares stocking.

5. No frills mean savings on non-essential items such as blankets, pillows, and hot meals. It also means being able to charge more on cash sales from those who need them as they can purchase the items on board the aircraft.

6. Reinforcing the low cost strategy, budget airlines sold their tickets via the internet. They therefore need not pay travel agent commission fees or computer reservations systems.

7. Flying to cheaper, less congested secondary airports and flying early in the morning or late in the evening to avoid air traffic delays and take advantage of lower landing fees.

8. Pilots and steward/stewardess doubled-up as cleaners and gate agents. Through performing in multiple roles, the airlines saved personnel costs.

From the numerous differentiators described above, it became apparent that the success of budget airline strategies is not contributed by a single product or service innovation. It is a well implemented and well orchestrated symphony of holistic business innovations aligned to a common clear strategy. Each product, services, frills, feature must reinforce the strategic direction (in this case is driving down cost and fast turnaround time) for the airline to be successful.

Great questions to ponder:

Key Point

What innovations can you drive such that each idea reinforces and is aligned to the overall strategic direction?

SUMMARY

Summary Notes

1. Leverage on project management methodology to implement your innovation project.

2. Make use of innovation techniques to brainstorm the various phases of project management to achieve the project objectives in the shortest possible time and using the least amount of resources.

3. Project Planning activities:
    a. Scope definition
    b. Activity definition
    c. Sequencing
    d. Resource planning
    e. Cost estimation/budgeting
    f. Quality planning
    g. Risk identification and management

4. Critical Success Factors – do these first!

5. Build prototypes to test the proof of concepts. Explore and experiment with different approaches, materials, or models.

6. Risk Management techniques: Risk Avoidance, Risk Reduction, Risk Transference, and Risk Acceptance.

7. Opportunity Management: Exploit, Enhance, Share, and Accept.

8. Take care of:
   a. Project related changes
   b. People related change management

9. Begin with an innovative business strategy. Ensure that each product or service innovation reinforces the overall business strategy. Throw away any projects that may conflict with the overall business objectives.

CHAPTER 11
ITERATION

"Iteration leads to continuous improvement."

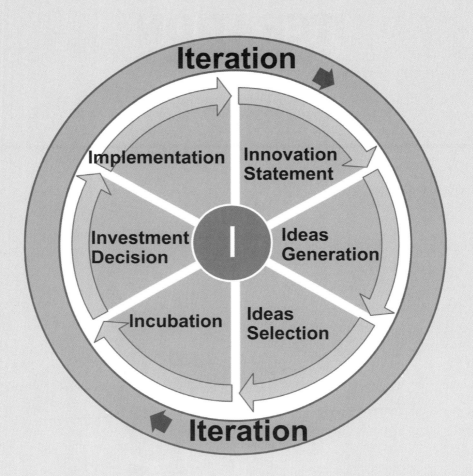

CHAPTER 11: ITERATION

When you are driving, do you constantly glance at your rear-view mirror and side mirrors although you are driving straight? You are checking and keeping yourself informed of the road conditions around you. During cross country driving, do you constantly look at the GPS screen although you are quite sure you are heading towards the right direction? You are reconfirming. Why are you doing that?

By keeping yourself informed about the road conditions and the traffic around you, you are able to react better should there be an emergency. Reconfirming your position on the GPS map every now and then gives you feedback of your current location and helps you detect early if you accidently took a wrong turn or deviated from your planned route. That's what iteration is about.

Iteration is the process of

► ALIGNMENT
  ■ It keeps checking and acting to keep your innovation project on track. From the initiation of the Innovation Statement to the Implementation phase, situations and conditions had changed. The project manager needs to make sure that that the objectives are still valid, the actions are still relevant, and the project is still on track. He will act to ensure the project stayed aligned to the business objectives.

► MONITORING
  ■ It focuses on measuring, monitoring, reporting, and reviewing. Iteration consists of these processes performed to observe project execution so that potential problems can be identified in a timely manner and corrective action can be taken, when necessary, to control the execution of the project. The key benefit is that project performance is observed and measured

regularly to identify variances from the project management plan.

▶ IMPROVING

- Throughout the innovation journey, the team learns about the tools and techniques and applies them to solve problems and obstacles encountered along the way. The team can use brainstorming techniques like SCAMPER repeatedly to generate ideas to overcome each obstacle and PCM to select the best ideas.

- By now, the team would have an innovative mindset to question, "Is there a better way?" repeatedly to continually improve the project. Plans get adjusted each time a new and better way is found.

- True iteration may bring the team back in circles as better and better ways are found. Exploit each idea as they appear and evaluate if the improvement is worth resetting that project phase.

Quality guru, Dr Edward Deming[67] , popularized the concept of Plan-Do-Check-Act cycle. The cycle iterates, and every time we revolve around a PDCA, we improve and fine-tune our products, our processes, and ourselves. Over time, we get better and more efficient.

▶ PLAN

- Establish the targets, objectives, and processes necessary to deliver results in accordance with the expected output.

▶ DO

- Execute the implementation plan to design and develop the innovative solution.

▶ CHECK

- Measure the new results derived from your innovation and

---

[67] The W. Edwards Deming Institute http://deming.org/

compare the results against the expected results to ascertain any differences.

▶ ACT
  ■ If deviation is detected, analyze the cause and take appropriate counteraction.

There are several questions to ponder during iteration:

1. Where are we going?
  ▶ This question defines the destination as stated in the Innovation Statement. It could be the vision statement, mission, objectives, and goals.
  ▶ Are our targets/goals still valid? Have they moved?
  ▶ We need to keep an eye on the development of the market, economy, competition, and technology. What makes sense for an innovation project a few months ago may already have been made obsolete by a competitive product. There's no point re-inventing the wheel when you can already buy one.

2. Where are we now?
  ▶ If the innovation project is about improving the current situation, environment, or process (e.g. operational efficiency, improvement of lead time, costs savings, etc), it is important to capture the original status of the situation BEFORE you embark on your innovation journey. This is called the Baseline Assessment. This original status served as the baseline that we can use to calculate the added value contributed by the innovation project.
  ▶ Brainstorm on what measures are appropriate for both the original and the new environment. Note that your innovation may make obsolete some of the current environment or process or the way your organization carries out its business.
    i.   What shall we measure?
    ii. How do we measure?
    iii. Can our existing tools collect the data required for our measurement?

▶ Wherever possible, choose a measure that can quantify the value contribution by your innovation in terms of dollar value. This is important for the justification of your investment.

3. How do we get there?
    ▶ The "How" is an action question that is answered by your implementation plan. During the iteration stage, we ask:
        i.   Is the plan still valid?
        ii. Is it moving in accordance to the plan? On time and budget? This is looking at the front, side, and back mirrors to make sure that we are on track.
        iii. Do I need to intervene to get the project back on track?

             If so, what corrective actions should I take?

             How can we get back on track?

             Who's involved in the corrective actions?

        iv. Can we get there cheaper? Faster? Safer? This is the continual improvement question to search for better solutions.

    ▶ How do I know where am I during my journey?
        i.   Monitoring: How to monitor and what to monitor?
        ii. Reporting: What reports should we generate? Who should we distribute the reports to?
        iii. Reviewing: Who should be in the review board? How frequently should we review?

4. How do I know that I have reached my destination?
    ▶ The destination/target should be defined BEFORE we embark on the journey. It serves as the beacon that guides our ship along the way.
    ▶ Logically, the destination should be clearly defined and is part of the measurement and reporting.
    ▶ To guide us to the destination, it is a good idea to define milestones along the way so that we know if we are on track.

CHAPTER 12
CONCLUSION

"Ideas can be turned into gold."

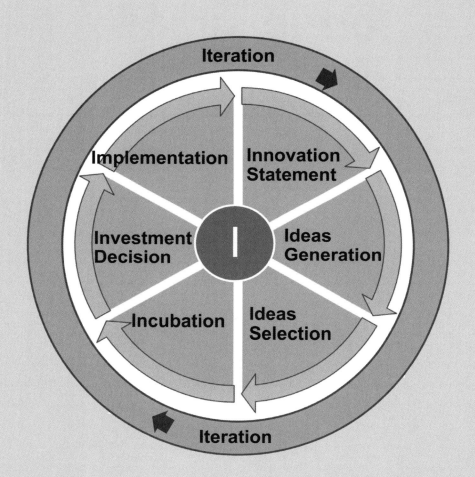

CHAPTER 12: CONCLUSION

SUNSHINE AFTER THE STORM: THE HP STORY

I began this book with an HP story. Having gone through the entire Wheel of Innovation, this is a good time to bring a close to the HP story. This concluding chapter helps you relate how you can apply the learning from the various chapters to your ideas into gold.

THE BATTLE OF JULU

… Continue from Page 22.

I remembered reading a book about the Battle of Julu[68] , Heibei, China in 207 B.C. After crossing a river, Rebel Commander Xiang Yu ordered the sinking of their ships, thereby committing his Chu army to defeat their enemy (Qin army), as there was no more means of returning home alive. Commander Xiang Yu further ordered his troops to carry only three days of ration and destroyed the remainder of the food supply and all their cooking utensils. This meant that his Chu army had to win the war within three days or they would all starve to death. Faced with no other means out of the situation, the Chu army fought fiercely despite being faced with a mightier enemy force.

To survive, they needed to win at all cost. As a result of total commitment, Xiang Yu's army of 30,000 Chu troops defeated the larger Qin army of 300,000 soldiers.

---

68 http://en.wikipedia.org/wiki/Battle_of_Julu

I had no ships to sink. The economic recession had sunk them all. I would want to protect my cooking pots, but the looming recession had threatened to destroy our rice bowls. Just like the Chu army, I had only one way to go – to survive, we needed to conquer the Asian Economic Crisis.

Back in the year 1997, in the midst of the Asian Economic Crisis, I had made a commitment to my Asia Pacific boss to lead my team out of recession. We had chosen to fulfill our revenue and profitability targets despite the recession. We had also chosen not to retrench any of our staff. In other words, we had chosen to cut costs to save jobs instead of cutting jobs to save cost.

Faced with this daunting task, I stayed awake for several nights trying to map out my course of action. Failure was not an option. It was the chance of our life to do what was right. It was our chance to change our destiny.

My key question was:

How to turn ideas into gold?

To survive through 1997/98, I needed millions of extra dollars to counter the effect of sliding currency rates and falling customer sales orders. I began to formulate the innovation framework, which I codenamed the "Wheel of Innovation." For each of the stages, I developed major steps that I would take and the tools/techniques that I should deploy. With the master plan in place, I was excited to get the Wheel of Innovation rolling.

Unlike the Chu army, I had more than three days. In US corporations, we are measured by the quarter. I reckoned that I needed to rally my team and put innovation to action within the first quarter, to achieve a breakeven by the second quarter, to bring in the profit by the third, and to exceed the whole year's revenue targets by the fourth quarter. To achieve this, we needed massive and decisive actions. We needed everyone to drive multiple projects to achieve the accumulated exponential snow-ball effect.

I was blessed with a united and capable management team. We had countless meetings and brainstorming sessions with the staff to generate ideas, to select ideas, and to implement them fast. Armed with the vision of "Best Service Center in the World", we began to transform our Service Center to embrace and exploit innovation.

FORMING THE S.W.A.T. TEAM

Acting as the overall Innovation Sponsor, I appointed each of my regional managers as Regional Innovation Owners to be accountable for the fulfillment of one of the regional KPIs, (Revenue, Profitability, Customer Satisfaction, Reseller Satisfaction, and Operational Efficiency).

I had six country service center managers reporting to me (Singapore, Malaysia, Thailand, Philippines, Indonesia, and Vietnam). In each of the countries, I worked with the country managers to appoint five Innovation Team leaders per country. Each Country Innovation Team Leader would lead an innovation team that focused on attaining their respective KPIs in their countries. The Country Innovation Team Leaders would report to the respective Regional Innovation Owners.

In Chapter 4, "Teaming for Innovation", I mentioned the need to have a Subject Matter Expert in your team. I was extremely fortunate to meet an energetic man, Ooi Tay Peng, the South East Asia Business Planning and Quality Manager. He was an expert in strategic planning, in quality and processes reengineering. With him as our Quality and Processes champion, we were ready to tear down walls, to reengineer the process, and to squeeze every drop of inefficiency out from the systems.

With the leaders in place, we travelled around the countries evangelizing our grand vision, garnering team members, gaining commitments, formulating action plans and training the management and staff on innovation.

COST-SAVING IDEAS

With hundreds of staff trained in innovation techniques like SCAMPER, PCM, and PENS, we had developed an interesting, positive, and creative working environment. Every morning, I got lots of emails on the new ideas, suggestions, and enhancements from my management and staff. Every day, we heard remarks like:

"How can we do this better?"

"Looking from the customers' perspectives, let's brainstorm some ideas on how we can overcome the following constraints."

"I have an idea to do … Can you give me a few suggestions on how to enhance this?"

Innovation permeated the air. Anyone stuck with a problem can randomly pull his colleagues into the conference room to brainstorm solutions. Because everyone was trained on innovation, idea generation was easy. Sometimes employees would pop into a brainstorming session randomly to contribute a few ideas on their way to the pantry. Sometimes a team leader would post an innovation statement on the notice board with a Post-It pad below, and by the next morning, he would get the whole notice board filled with ideas from passing colleagues. An idea spawned a thousand other ideas. Good ideas got enhanced and built upon to create brilliant ideas. Soon, excitement burst into actions.

FREE SPARE PARTS IDEA

As I was looking for money-saving ideas, I asked my financial analyst, Kelli Yao, to go through with me every high cost expense item. Clearly, for my service and support industry, our heaviest expense cost item was people cost. As we had promised not to retrench anyone, we moved on to the second highest cost item, which was logistics.

Key Point

If you want to save a few million dollars from expenses, where do you start?

You start with the biggest expense item to trim.

My logistics manager, Eddy Ngiam, briefed me that there were two major components that made up the logistics cost:

1. The cost of spare parts consumed
2. The cost of flying these parts around the world

The need to reduce the two major cost components in logistics triggered the following innovation statements, each of them assigned to an innovation team:

▶ How to minimize the overall cost of logistics?

▶ How to minimize the consumption of spares?

▶ How to reduce the number of spares consumed per repair job?

▶ How can we minimize/avoid the freight charges?

During one of the team's brainstorming session, the team generated a thousand cost-saving ideas for logistics. They used the Perspectives-Criteria Matrix to select the best idea with the maximum savings. One idea that emerged top was, **"Get Free Spares Parts"**.

At the first glance, one would reject an idea like "free spare parts" as crazy. We were not concerned about getting one or two pieces free to save us pennies. We were dealing with ideas that would save us millions of dollars per year. Certainly, it would be absurd to expect millions of dollars worth of spare parts to be available free of charge.

What we needed was a change in mindset. Creativity is not just about thinking differently. It is about the ability perceive the impossible as possible, then to actively seek out solutions to make the possible happen. Instead of rejecting crazy ideas, we should ask, "How to?" and, "Where can we find free spares parts?"

While researching for innovation ideas, we stumbled on an interesting article about the recycling of bio-waste into energy products. The two keywords "recycling" and "waste" caught our attention. The word "Waste" has close relationship with the word "Free". Out of curiosity, we asked:

"What are the wastes coming out from our HP factories?"

"What happened to these wastes?"

Pondering through the word "waste", we probed through a series of structured questions. One question led to another, each question spawning off a few more interesting questions.

"How did the HP factories deal with product rejects?"

"Did the HP factories simply throw their assembled products away because they failed the final quality tests?"

"Or did they repair and recycle these rejects?"

We began to see a possibility of recycling these factory rejects in our service center. We could strip the products into modules, discard the faulty modules, and salvage the good ones as our spare parts.

While on the topic of recycling faulty products and rejects, we asked:

"What else?", "Where else?" and, "Who else?"

"Which other product divisions?"

"Which other processes?"

Using the trigger word "Reverse" and "Rearrange" in the SCAMPER brainstorming technique, we asked what happened before the HP products reached our service center. The product sales process preceded the service support process. On the whiteboard, we outlined the process flow from the factory to the channel partners to the retailers, and finally to the end consumer. Then we tried to reverse the flow and traced it from the consumer and back.

Then we asked the question, "What happens when the product failed upon arrival or when the customers rejected/returned the product for whatever reasons?" They couldn't be resold, as the boxes may have been torn open, the plastic covers dirtied, and the items within no longer brand new. How did these rejected products get flown back to the factory?

We could not find the answer. Factories are very good in assembling products, but they were not designed to repair or dissemble rejected products. No matter how good HP product quality was, we were certain that there were a small percentage of rejected products. A small percentage of rejected products out of a few million manufactured products a month would be several thousand pieces for us each month. If these rejected products did not come to the service center (that's us) for repair, and it was not logical for the factories to repair them, where did they go? If we could find the source of these returned products, we would have found our gold mine of free spare parts. We were intrigued.

Under the capable leadership of Quality Manager, the innovation team embarked upon the journey to solve the mystery of the missing rejected products. We traced the process around the world and found that all the Asia Pacific returned products ended up with an Administration Manager located in Singapore. And that Admin Manager sat in another building just a few kilometers from us.

We got very excited. Quickly we arranged to meet up with him. What do you think an Admin Manager would do with the returned products? An Admin Manager did admin paper work of course! His job was to scrap the products and send them to the dump yard! We could not believe it. Container-loads of our precious potential spare parts dumped every month.

The innovation team worked with the Admin Manager to redirect these container-loads of returned products to our service center each month. At our service center, we provide extensive training to teams of polytechnic student interns (you guess it – cheap, eager, and brilliant labor force) to strip the returned products into their modules sub-assemblies. They tested each module, threw away the faulty ones, repacked the good modules into brown boxes and labeled them. Viola!

We had created a gold mine with continuous flowing supply of free spare parts.

From the success of this "Get Free Spare Parts" idea alone, our team was able to save millions of dollars worth of spare parts expenses. We now had enough money to pay the salaries of all our staff, plus a lot more spare cash to invest in infrastructure (whereupon we launched 12 brand new service centers in Thailand in the middle of the economic recession).

REVENUE GENERATING IDEAS

To be highly profitable, a business needs to fix its top line (grow the revenue) and its bottom line (reduce costs). Let's explore what ideas we had to grow ourselves out of recession.

Growth Idea 1:

Using "Combine" in SCAMPER, we generated an idea to combine services (my business) with the products (another division's business). During that time, HP had a service called SupportPack (today, it is known as Care Pack[69]), which was a service to upgrade the warranty from one year to three year. The SupportPack was sold through resellers. However, due to product price competition, resellers were reluctant to sell SupportPacks together with the products. Only 5% of our customers purchased them (this was known as the penetration rate).

The idea generated by the team was to bundle the SupportPack with a product line of printers sold. This meant that that all the printers sold for that selected product line would be bundled with three years warranty. Bundling extended warranty by product line eliminated a lot of cost elements, like:

▶ Resellers' commission for the sale of SupportPacks
▶ Printing, transportation, and warehousing costs of the physical SupportPacks
▶ All administrative work pertaining to the data entry and tracking of customer information on the SupportPacks

With the bulk of commissions, printing, storage, and administration costs eliminated, it worked out that we could support the extended three-year warranty with a mere increment of just 2% of the product price. A $100

---

[69] http://www.hp.com/

printer could be sold for $102 with three years warranty.

This innovative packaging threw the competitors off-guard. With only 2% price difference, customers loved the three years warranty, which the competitors could not give. HP sold a lot more products, services (my business) grew a lot more in revenue, and customers loved us. A simple act of bundling increased our services penetration rate from 5% to 100%. It's a win-win-win formula that brought in the extra million dollars and propelled our growth.

Growth Idea 2:

Remember our "Free Spare Parts" cost reduction program? That program was so successful that it not only provided free spare parts for our own consumption, there were a lot more spares piling up and over spilling the capacity of my logistic warehouse. When a customer rejected a personal computer (e.g. it could not boot up from Day 1), only one module was bad. But the good monitor, keyboard, mouse, hard disks all ended up in our logistic stores as spares. We had thousands of good hard disks, memory chips, motherboards, mice, and monitors stacked up high from floor to ceiling.

What could we do with them?

Sell them for more money of course!

We sold lots of these excess spares to other HP logistics centers (for internal expense relief) and launched a sales program to sell these spares to resellers, repair shops, hobbyists, students, etc. We generated another powerful profitable stream of revenue out of our Free Spare Parts Program.

Growth Idea 3:

What made us proud of our innovation effort was that many of the great growth ideas came from our junior front counter staff. Being a service center, our traditional mindset was to service products after they **had failed**, and that we would not earn money from warranty customers.

Through innovation (reverse thinking), we launched numerous programs that earned revenue:

▶ From products that did not fail:
  ▪ Upgrading/sale of memory and hard disk capacity
  ▪ Selling of extra power adapters (because you need one at home, one in the office, and one more for travel)

  (Guess where these memory chips, hard disks, and adaptors came from.)

▶ From services that were traditionally none of our business (out-of-the-box thinking). We observed our customers and it was clear that our customers needed help in the following "chores":
  ▪ Disk and system optimization services
  ▪ Virus removal service
  ▪ Printing services on large format printers
  ▪ Data backup and recovery service, etc

Besides the four project ideas illustrated above, the innovation teams across all six countries had generated and implemented hundreds of ideas, both big and small. Some failed miserably while some succeeded wildly. At every corner, from every opportunity and with every transaction, the teams innovated and implemented ideas that saved and grew money. Very soon, our revenue and profitability turned from red ink to pink, and then blue ink emerged. Innovation projects produced results and snowballed. Profitability rung and champagne poured.

THE EVEREST SUMMIT

The journey took us eighteen months, from my telephone conversation with my Asia Pacific boss to the ending of HP's Fiscal Year 1998. In the midst of the dark recession and currency turmoil, we had chosen to brave the storm. We got wet, bruised, and almost drowned. But we emerged triumphant.

To recap, the Indonesia Rupiah had plunged to 13.5% of its original value versus the US dollar and the Thai Baht plunged to 25.8%. Mathematically, this meant that we needed to grow our revenue to 740% in terms of local rupiah and 386% in terms of baht just to reach our 100% revenue target in US dollars.

And we did. We not only did hit 100%, we surpassed it to a heroic average height of 150% revenue US$ target in all six countries in every of my six business product lines. Our profitability target was 4% (reduced from 8% by my kind boss). We hit a dazzling and embarrassing height of 40% profit. It was embarrassing because we made our colleagues from the other departments and our friendly competitors (IBM, SUN, etc) feel bad. They were all drowning in the red ocean!

With so much profit overflowing our piggy banks, we had more than enough money to invest in building infrastructure, in customer satisfaction programs, in reseller programs, in staff trainings, and in innovation incentives. To motivate the various innovation teams to reach their targets, we initiated The Everest Challenge where teams who had reached their innovation targets were given trophies and cash prizes.

Our investments in customer satisfaction programs and reseller programs paid off as we were conferred the "Best in Service & Support" by Computer World magazine Readers' Choice Award[70] and the "Best in

---

[70] http://www.computerworld.com.sg/

Reseller Satisfaction" by Channels Asia Magazine. With each of the KPIs fulfilled, we had accomplished our dream to be the Best Service Center in the World.

We had set forth to achieve the impossible; we had achieved the impossible.

Looking back, this story happened more than 10 years ago. Innovation changed my life – and the lives of everyone involved with the Everest Challenge. I left HP in 2001 to form my own training and consulting company (Everest Innovation Pte Ltd[71] – no prize for guessing how my company got her name) to share the secrets of innovation with the world. On numerous occasions, I bumped into my colleagues in HP. In the café or the airport lounges, we would chat over our good old 1997/98 days. Those days were memorable.

We had left behind a legacy. In our spirits and in our minds, we are no longer constrained by the traditional thinking around us.

If we can conquer the economic recession, what other forces can we not conquer?

If we can generate 1000 ideas in half hour, what problems can we not solve?

We are what we know.

We are what we can do or achieve.

We can become who we want to be.

The future is for us to create.

Create a legacy today.

---

[71] http://www.everesti.com/

SUMMARY

Summary Notes

Learning from "Get Free Spare Parts" story:

► Treat all ideas as good ideas, no matter how stupid, crazy, or weird.

► Crazy ideas can be turned into world-class innovation.

► Waste can be turned into gold.

► Look for waste, across departments, across geography.

► When you've found waste and found a means to recycle, reuse, and refresh them, you've found a gold mine.

Learning from revenue generating stories:

► Look out for ideas to COMBINE and to leverage on the strength of your company or the other product divisions.

► Bundle things together to achieve 100% penetration rate for maximum growth impact with minimum costs.

► Sell products and services BEFORE, DURING, and AFTER your traditional customer needs.

► Look out for customers' chores. These are areas they would gladly pay you to get them done.

BIBLIOGRAPHY

Andrew Read, M. T. (2009, Jan 2). *Microbiology: Mosquitoes Cut Short. Science Magazine.*

Barthelemy, D. B. (1997). *The Sky is Not the Limit. St. Lucie Press.*

Canton, James (2007) *The Extreme Future: The Top Trends that will reshape the world in the next 20 years. Penguin Group.*

Christensen, T. B. (2005). *Creative Cognition: Analogy and Incubation. University of Aarhus, Denmark.*

Covey, Stephen. (2003). *The 7 Habits of Highly Effective People. Simon & Schuster.*

Dell, Michael. w. (1999). *Direct from DELL. Harper Collins Fredman.*

Deming, *The W. Edwards Deming Institute http://deming.org/.*

Drucker, P. F. (1954). *The Practice of Management.*

DSTA. (2005). *Development & Deployment of Infrared Fever Screening Systems by Tan Yang How and Team. https://www.dsta.gov.sg/index.php/DSTA-2005-Chapter-1/.*

Dweck, C. S. (2006). *Mindset: The new psychology of success. USA: Random House.*

Eberle, Bob. (1997). *SCAMPER: Creative Games and Activities for Imagination Development. Prufrock Press.*

Everest (IMAX) [Motion Picture]. *A MacGillivray Freeman Flim (1996). Greene, K. a. (1998). The Story of Walt Disney. Viking.*

International Project Management Association, *www.ipma.ch.*

Jack, K. Gunpowder: Alchemy, Bombards, and Pyrotechnics: the History of Explosive that Changed the World. New York: Basic Books, Perseus Books Group.

Jomo, K. e. (1997). Southeast Asia's Msunderstood Miracle: Industrial Policy and Economic Development in Thailand, Malaysia and Indonesia. Boulder, CO: Westview Press.

Jomo, K. e. (1998). Tigers in Trouble: Financial Governance, Liberalisation and Crises in East Asia. London, UK: Zed Books.

Karunatilleka, E. (1999, 11 Feb). Asian Economic Crisis. House of Commons. UK: House of Commons Library.

Kuan, S. (2006). RFID What went right? What went wrong? Bibliotheksdienst 40. Jg. (2006), H. 8/9 .

Michalko, Michael. (2006). Thinkertoys: A handbook of creative thinking techniques (2nd Edition). Ten Speed Press.

Ministry of Information Communication and the Arts, Singapore. (2004). A Defining Moment: How Singapore beat SARS. Singapore: Stamford Press Pte Ltd.

O'Neill, S., McMeniman, C., Lane, R., Cass, B., Fong, A., & Wang, M. S. (2009, Jan 2). Stable Introduction of a Life-Shortening Wolbachia Infection into mosquito Aede aegypti. Science Magazine , pp. 141-144.

Packard, D. (1995). The HP Way: How Bill Hewlett and I Build Our Company. New York: HarperCollins.

Project in Controlled Environment, PRINCE2. www.ogc.gov.uk/prince2. Project Management Institute. (2004). Guide to the Project Management Body of Knowledge. www.pmi.org.

Reflections on the Asian Crisis, Vol 3, No 3. (1998). Journal of Asa Pacific Economy.

Spector, R. (2000). Amazon.com, Get Big Fast. Harper Business.

Stoddard, D. (2006, July 14). Fireworks: safer than candles, tableware. Sacramento Ledger Dispatch.

Straits Times, (2009, Jan 3). Dengue: Science bites back. Straits Time.

Straits Time. (2005, Aug 24). 24-hour call centre – behind bars.

Straits Time. (2005, July 29). Sweet Female Voice on hotline.

Straits Times, (1993, March 31). Electronic Vaulting Service. Safe as a Bank? , p. SS4.

TIME. (2003). Coolest Invention of the Year 2003. http://www.time.com/time/2003/inventions/invaquada.html.

TIME. (2003). Coolest Invention 2003. http://www.time.com/time/2003/inventions/invfever.html.

Walt Disney Company. (2004, june 28). Disney debuts new safer, quieter and more environmentally-friendly fireworks technology. Press release.

World Health Organization. (2006). SARS: How a global epidemic was stopped. WHO Press.

WEBSITE REFERENCES

http://en.beijing2008.cn/
http://en.wikipedia.org/wiki/All-in-one
http://en.wikipedia.org/wiki/American Inventor (2006)
http://en.wikipedia.org/wiki/American Inventor (2007)
http://en.wikipedia.org/wiki/American Inventor (n.d.)
http://en.wikipedia.org/wiki/Battle_of_Julu
http://en.wikipedia.org/wiki/Dengue
http://en.wikipedia.org/wiki/Dick_Fosbury
http://en.wikipedia.org/wiki/Greg_Chavez
http://en.wikipedia.org/wiki/Janusz_Liberkowski
http://en.wikipedia.org/wiki/Laser_printer
http://inventorspot.com/update_on_the_anecia_survival_casule
http://www.3m.com/
http://www.best-management-practice.com/IT-Service-Management-ITIL/
http://www.dell.com/
http://www.ducktours.com.sg/ducktours.html
http://www.eurocopter.ca/asp/cmNews050524.asp
http://www.everesti.com/
http://www.gibbstech.co.uk/aquada.php
http://www.hp.com/
http://www.ideafinder.com/history/inventions/postit.htm
http://www.itil-officialsite.com/home/home.asp
http://www.mounteverest.net/news.php?id=1327
http://www.nlb.gov.sg/
http://www.ryanair.com/
http://www.southwest.com/

INDEX

TRAINING WORKSHOPS

Our portfolio of innovation workshops is as follows:

A) Turning Ideas into Gold: Essentials

This is an introductory two-day workshop covering the essentials of how to embrace innovation to turn ideas into gold.
It covers the essential topics on:

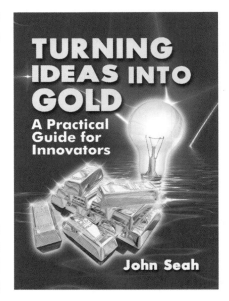

- Innovative Mindset
- Innovation Statement
- Ideas Generation
- Ideas Selection
- Incubation

The key "WOW" factor of this workshop is that the participants should be able to **generate 1000 ideas in 28 minutes!** The emphasis is on the phases of Ideas Generation and Ideas Selection.

B) Turning Ideas into Gold: Management

This two-day workshop is designed for the management team to lead their team from the Innovation Statement phase to the Investment Decision.

It covers all the essential phases, presented from the management perspectives and with emphasis on the formulation of the Innovation Statement and on making Investment Decisions.

C) Turning Ideas into Gold: Selling Ideas

This is an optional one-day add-on workshop to Workshops (A) and (B). It focuses on how to sell your innovation ideas to senior management or judges. This is ideal if you are preparing your team for innovation competitions or for presentation to senior management for their support and funding.

D) Turning Ideas into Gold: Facilitator

This is a three-day workshop program designed for companies who want to groom their participants to be facilitators for the "Turning Ideas into Gold" program and to guide their own participants through the innovation journey.

E) Turning Ideas into Gold: The Everest Challenge

This is a comprehensive organization–wide program for companies who want to lead their teams from the conception of the idea to the fruition of the innovation. It consists of a series of workshops, consulting, hand-holding, and coaching sessions for the management team and the participants.

For enquiries, contact: **johnseah@everesti.com**
Website: **www.everesti.com**